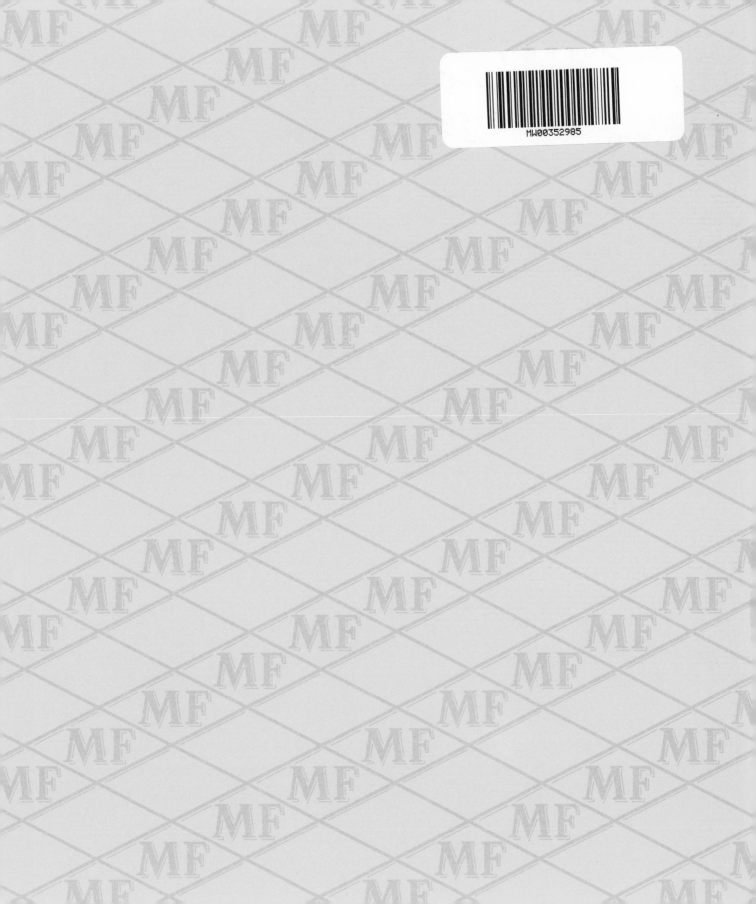

MARIAGE FRÈRES
FRENCH TEA

Three Centuries of Savoir-Faire

1182 DARJEELING
BANNOCKBURN
FTGFOP1

1183 DARJEELING
PHOOBSERING
FTGFOP1

119
TEEST

1270 DARJEELING
DARJEELING impérial
SFTGFOP1

128 DARJEELING
MASTER
TGFOP

129
PRI

120 DARJEELING POOBONG FTGFOP

ALAIN STELLA

M A R I A G E   F R È R E S
FRENCH TEA

Three Centuries of Savoir-Faire

Photography by
Francis Hammond

Flammarion

130 DARJEELING RAJAH TGFOP

141 DARJEELING ARYA

Editorial direction
Suzanne Tise-Isoré

Graphic design and art direction
Bernard Lagacé
and Nils Herrmann

Translated from the French by
Deke Dusinberre

Copyediting and proofreading
Christine Schultz-Touge

Color separation
Quat'coul, Toulouse
Les artisans du Regard, Paris

Printing
Zanardi, Italy

Distributed in North America
by Rizzoli International Publications, Inc.

Simultaneously published in French as
Thé français, trois siècles de passion
© Flammarion, SA, Paris and
Mariage Frères, 2003/2009

English-language edition
© Flammarion, SA, Paris and
Mariage Frères, 2003/2009

09 10 11 4 3 2
ISBN: 978-2-08-011176-0
Dépôt légal: 10/2003
Printed in Italy by Zanardi

RIGHT
The tearoom and emporium on
Rue du Bourg-Tibourg in Paris.

CONTENTS

TOP, FROM LEFT TO RIGHT

Gyokuro, Brumes d'Himalaya, Opium Hill

BOTTOM, FROM LEFT TO RIGHT

Yin Zhen, Yunnan d'Or, Neige de Jade

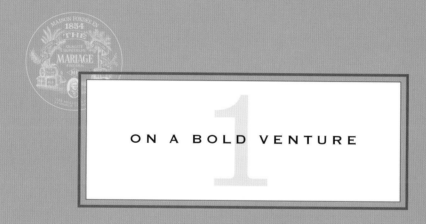

1

ON A BOLD VENTURE

O pen the door of the Mariage Frères tea house, and a mysterious fragrance slyly declares itself. This fragrance comes forward first to greet you, then embrace you. From that moment onward, the scent will have seduced you completely. It is all the more bewitching for being unlike any other smell, for promising unknown adventure. Other perfumes can be described as either fruity, or earthy, or woody, or any of the countless adjectives commonly used in such cases. But not in this instance. It's a scent, that's all you can say—a very special scent, an unfamiliar perfume, a dreamy fragrance. Yet it's so caressing and voluptuous that you might be tempted to say, like everyone else who vainly attempts to describe it, that it's the scent of paradise. To a certain extent, this fragrance incarnates the spirit of Mariage Frères. The French tea merchant launches you on a sensual voyage to a dream-like place, unique in the world, full of endless delights. Mariage Frères invites you to discover its wealth of five hundred teas, each of which, on being served, yields up a few molecules of scent certain to surprise and charm you.

Standing on the threshold of paradise, you look around. You have opened the door to number 30 Rue du Bourg-Tibourg in the Marais district of Paris, near the old center of town. Inaugurated on August 1, 1985, this is the oldest of Mariage Frères' five tea houses—three in Paris, two in Tokyo. Long-time regulars who were familiar with the firm's old warehouse and outlet on Rue du Cloître-Saint-Merri recognize most of the features: the many wooden furnishings such as the long oak counter where tea is sold, the little glassed office where the cashier now sits, and—most importantly—the exotic charm that creates an impression of voyaging in space and time. Nowadays, however, thanks to the company's considerable fame, customers crowd around the counter while a brigade of clerks, all tea specialists, dressed in beige linen suits, bustles in front of an extraordinary display of tea: hundreds of large black tea canisters nestle in a wonderful checkerboard of wooden cubicles. A canister is pulled down and opened for a customer. The clerk draws out a fistful of tea with a brass scoop for examination and then weighs the tea on an old set of scales. Above the scales rises a diaphanous cloud of tea—a few milligrams of Ambootia, Silver Dragon, or Opium Hill. It all forms a poetic, artful choreography so pleasant and scented that you never weary of it. While awaiting their turn, customers can also inspect the various teapots sold in the tea house, including cast-iron versions from Japan and earthenware models from

Yixing in China, specially devised by Mariage Frères' owners during their travels but now imitated throughout the world.

If you penetrate still further into this realm of tea, you will come upon a tearoom and restaurant bathed in daylight softly filtered through a glass roof. While sitting in a wicker chair, surrounded by colorful bouquets of philodendron, heliconia, and pandanus, and served by a waiter dressed in white linen, you can easily imagine yourself on the veranda of a colonial residence or on the deck of an Asian liner off the coast of Vietnam or India. Soft notes of classical music swirl through the room, almost inducing a sense of nostalgia—you are already a long way from Paris, and your mind fills with faraway images as your palate samples exotic delights: a "coup de soleil" Crème Brûlée, a Mount Fuji Mousse made with green Matcha tea, or Chandernagor Chocolate Cake. These desserts might be accompanied by a pot of exotic Aventurier tea, a smoky Grand Manchu blend from China, or a fine first-flush Darjeeling. You probably thought you were indulging in an experience that would last an hour—but now you sense that it will last a lifetime.

Still wrapped in this cloud of sensations, on leaving the table you can head upstairs to the Mariage Frères Tea Museum. It will transport you back to the days when this adventure all began. Here the Mariage family's personal collection has been enriched by items acquired more recently, revealing the extent to which the world of tea has given birth to an entire realm of decorative art: old painted crates for shipping the tea by sea, ornamental boxes—the famous tea caddies—of bygone centuries, and precious tea services of all kinds from all lands. There are also mementos of the Mariage firm in the nineteenth century, such as account books, invoices, old labels, and photos of the shops and offices of yore. The museum evokes the very dawn of the history of the Mariage Frères company. Take the model of a majestic three-masted ship. It might just be the *Fils de France,* christened in Nantes in April 1818 and outfitted for the "China trade," from whence it regularly returned—for decades on end—with tons of tea, cinnamon, silk, and even mandarin oranges. Some of these exotic products were sold by the Mariage family, merchants from Lille who began in the "Eastern trade" back in the seventeenth century. Indeed, the scent of paradise that rises to the upper floor of the museum also contains a whiff of three centuries of travel and adventure.

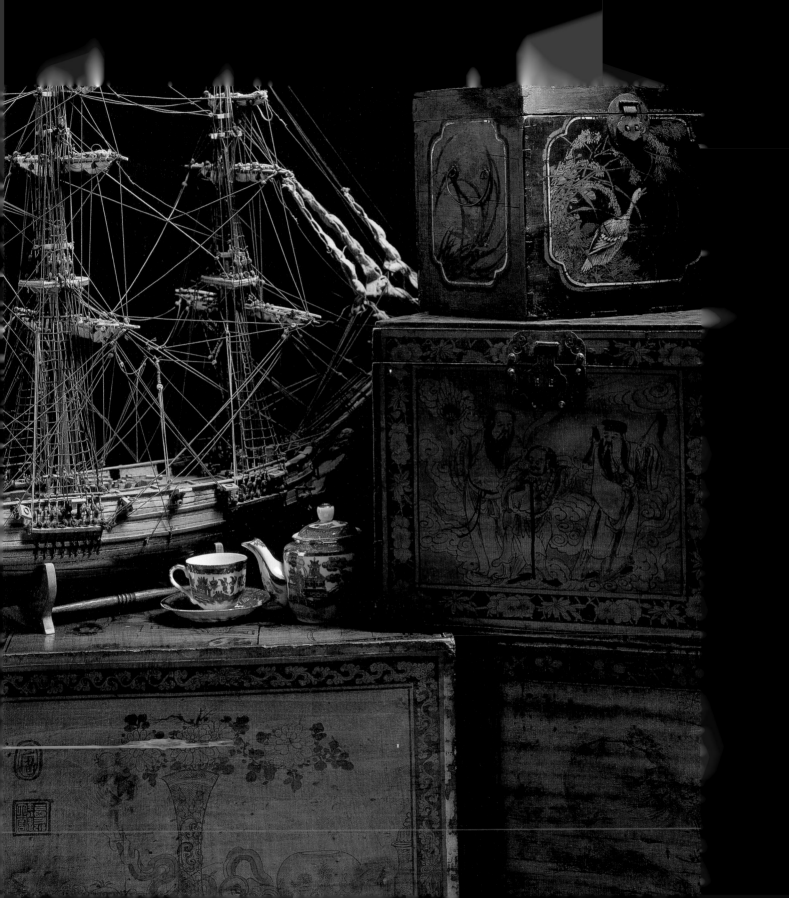

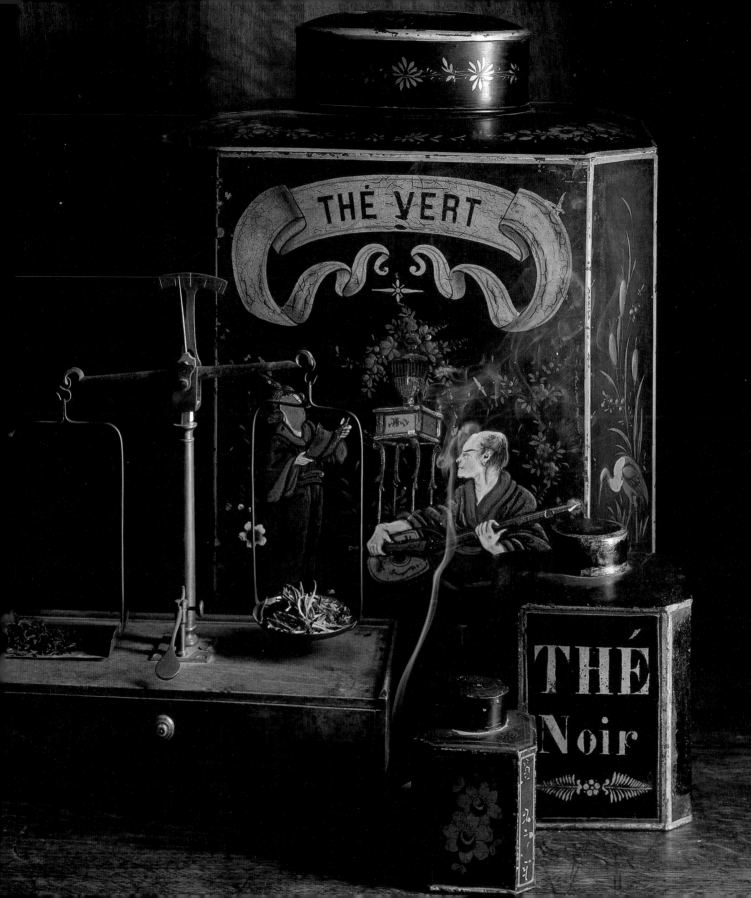

LEFT *Other treasures in the Mariage Frères museum include these tea canisters dating from the 19th century, when the firm was founded. The largest one illustrates the fact that the first tea imported into Europe was green tea (thé vert), only later overshadowed by black tea (thé noir).* RIGHT *The frontispiece of Philippe Sylvestre Dufour's "Traités nouveaux & curieux du Café, du Thé et du Chocolate", the first French book on the exotic products of coffee, tea, and chocolate. It was a best-seller when published in 1671.*

TRAITÉS NOVVEAVX & CVRIEVX DV CAFÉ DV THÉ ET DV CHOCOLATE
Composéz
Par Philippe Sylvestre Dufour

Voyages seem to be in the Mariage family blood, if the etymology of the name is anything to go by. Contrary to expectation, the name has nothing to do with marriage or nuptials of any kind. It comes from the old French verb *maréier,* "to run the seas," *mer* being French for sea. In a nautical context, a *maréage* was a sailor's contract for the run, that is to say a set wage for a given voyage regardless of how long it lasted. A number of related nouns and adjectives once existed in French, such as *marage* and *maraige.* Thus prior to 1650 the family name was spelled in different ways, according to various birth certificates: Marage, Maroige, Mariage, and Maraige. It was only after 1650 that Mariage was permanently adopted. The family's more remote roots extend back to the thirteenth century, in the Hainaut region of Flanders where the coat of arms of the viscounts of Maraige bore a "barry of six or and gules on a chief of the second a fleur-de-lys of the first." The earliest Mariage on the current genealogical tree was Hugues de Maraige, a crusader to the Holy Land. Four centuries later came the first Mariages to specialize in the trade of exotic goods, namely Pierre and Nicolas Mariage, two of the four sons of a royal forestry superintendent in Normandy. In the 1660s, Pierre was sent to Madagascar on a mission for the French East India Company, while Nicolas made several trips to Persia and India before being named part of an official deputation sent by Louis XIV to sign a trade agreement with the Shah of Persia. "Distant trade" was henceforth part of the family tradition, and the Mariage brothers were most probably already interested in tea.

Once Cardinal Mazarin—who drank tea to cure his gout—became a powerful minister at the French court in 1639, the beverage enjoyed great popularity within wealthy French circles. The Mariages were among the dealers who imported and sold it. At the time, people drank green tea from China, which was also the source of fine porcelain, silks, and spices. The French then began importing tea directly on the ships of the French East India Company, founded by the government in 1664. Large three-masted ships

Ever since the British crown dispatched Robert Fortune to China to uncover the mystery of tea, China has striven to keep the secrets of its finest teas under wraps. These exclusive teas, symbols of honor and prestige, still remain inaccessible to anyone unwilling to deploy a great deal of diplomacy, persuasion, and patience.

RIGHT *In the latter half of the 19th century, Mariage Frères was supplier to the famous Paris tea shop, A la Porte Chinoise, which served as a meeting place for "orientalist" writers and painters such as Emile Zola and Edouard Manet (Manet's portrait of Zola is pictured here). They may have sampled Chocolat des Mandarins, a tea-flavored chocolate launched by Henri Mariage in 1860.*

spent a year on the high seas, and sailors faced extreme dangers ranging from typhoons to strange diseases. There was no guarantee they would ever see home again. So every day they prayed for safe return, their ship's hold being full of costly goods that would enable them to enjoy a small fortune until their next run began. Despite the vagaries of this distant trade, the tinkle of silver spoons in porcelain cups never abated at the French court and in the salons of Paris. While the tea itself was usually the same, and while it was drunk above all for medicinal reasons, the services in which this highly fashionable beverage was served outdid one another in magnificence. That is why the finest porcelain artists in France, at the manufactories of Vincennes and Sèvres, mobilized all their talent to create teapots, cups, sugar bowls, and utensils, as did the best goldsmiths in the kingdom. The likes of Chancellor Séguier, Madame de Genlis, Racine, and the marquise de Sévigné were fervent fans of tea, doing their best to make this new ceremony a pleasurable event conducive to conversation. Tea thus became, alongside chocolate, one of the main aristocratic pleasures. England experienced a similar infatuation—Catherine of Braganza, queen consort of King Charles II, transmitted her passion for tea to the court of Saint James. Unlike France, however, tea began filtering down to less aristocratic circles in England by the second half of the seventeenth century, thanks to "coffee houses" where it was served. So tea soon became an integral part of the English lifestyle.

Mariage family chronicles offer little information about the century following the expeditions of brothers Pierre and Nicolas. But we know that their sons and grandsons pursued the trade in exotic goods, and that the family tradition was maintained by Jean-François Mariage, born in 1766. Jean-François was a merchant in Lille who sold tea, spices, and other colonial goods. He trained his four sons—Louis, Aimé, Charles, and Auguste—in the trade. Around 1820, the three elder brothers formed a company to succeed their father. The youngest, Auguste, aged barely twenty, left for Paris to work for a sugar refiner. He then set up his own colonial goods firm in 1830 on Rue Simon-le-Franc, thereby becoming the first member of the Mariage family to hang his shingle in the Marais district of Paris. The three other brothers had split up two years earlier; Charles joined Auguste in Paris, while Aimé and Louis remained in Lille. Both of these

latter men continued to deal in colonial products—Louis also opened a sugar refinery, while Aimé specialized in new-fangled candles made of stearine (called "Northern candles") and in the tastier product of table chocolate (including a vanilla-flavored variety). According to family legend, as recounted by his grandson Henri, Aimé was overwhelmed by the workload and neglected the financially riskier products—he tried to concentrate on turning his suffering retail trade around. Finally, heavily in debt, he decided to shut his shop in Lille in 1843, and left for Paris with wife and eleven children, joining forces with brothers Auguste and Charles, who bought his factory in Lille. Business was sufficiently prosperous to allow Auguste and Charles to move from Rue Simon-le-Franc to larger premises at 23 Rue Sainte-Croix-de-la-Bretonnerie. Aimé became the chief clerk, while his sons Aimé junior, Henri, and Édouard, aged fifteen to seventeen, joined the firm as simple employees. The route from work to home was not far, since on arrival in Paris Aimé moved his family into a second-floor apartment on Rue du Bourg-Tibourg, overlooking the street. They lived there for seven years before moving to Rue de la Verrerie, unaware that one day their name would make little Rue du Bourg-Tibourg famous throughout the world.

It was around this time that Charles, his fortune made, retired from the business. In 1845, Auguste and Aimé renamed the firm Auguste Mariage & Company. They parted ways eight years later, subsequent to family disputes, and the company was dissolved. Aimé then went into the oil trade, while Auguste went into business with one of his employees, Guérin, tacking the name of his youngest son, Ernest, onto the new firm—Ernest Mariage Fils, Guérin, & Compagnie.

One year later, in 1854, Aimé's three sons went into businesses of their own. Aimé junior was established as a broker by his Uncle Auguste, while Henri and Édouard founded, on June 1st, the tea and vanilla import firm, Mariage Frères, that still exists today. For over 130 years it was headquartered on Rue du Cloître-Saint-Merri, just a few yards from the current Pompidou Center. The family lived on the same street, at number 4, just above the warehouse and office—the latter were subsequently transferred across the street, to number 3-b. Édouard died prematurely in 1890, and his sons went into different professions. Alone at the head of the company, Henri later handed the reins to his son, another Henri (born in 1872), and his son-in-law, Léon Cottin (husband of Marie Mariage). It was one of Léon and Marie's daughters, Marthe Cottin, born in 1901, who was the last member of the family to run the business, until 1983.

These three generations turned Mariage Frères into France's most glamorous tea merchant. They did not buy tons of leaves destined for industrial use, but rather imported costly teas, plus vanilla, which they sold to grand hotels and fine food stores. In the late nineteenth century, Mariage Frères basically sold the finest black teas from China, including smoky souchongs, as well as the early varieties from India and Ceylon, notably the long-leaf orange pekoe teas that would become its specialty (called "vermicelli leaf" within the firm). The company's prestigious clients, for whom it also devised exclusive

blends, included the Ritz and George V hotels, the Ladurée Tea Salon, the Faguais and Corcellet fine food stores, and the exclusive food sector of Printemps Department Store. (To simplify things, Mariage Frères gave its various blends a number, and this numbering system, now over one hundred years old, still survives in the current catalogue.) Starting in the 1860s, Mariage Frères also supplied a famous store on Rue Vivienne that retailed Far Eastern goods, namely A la Porte Chinoise, where the orientophile literary and artistic crowd would meet—the likes of Edmond and Jules de Goncourt, Charles Baudelaire, and Émile Zola, not to mention Claude Monet, Édouard Manet, Édgar Degas, and Henri Fantin-Latour. At la Porte Chinoise they could not only buy lacquerware, porcelain, and prints, they could also drink delicious China tea while talking of art and literature. Nor were tea and vanilla the only products sold by Mariage Frères—in 1860, Henri had imitated his father, Aimé, by entering the chocolate business. He launched Mariage Frères' first tea-flavored gourmet delight—a "superfine" chocolate, dubbed Chocolat des Mandarins,

BELOW *A late 19th-century receipt for a delivery of tea shipped by train.*
RIGHT *An early 20th-century label for tea selected and prepared by Mariage Frères for one of its clients.*

flavored with "superior quality" tea. Still reflecting the medicinal approach so fashionable since the seventeenth century, Henri's new product was promoted for its digestive virtues rather than its delicious taste.

By the early 1980s, Mariage Frères was certainly a venerable institution, but it remained unknown to the general public. Out of its Rue du Cloître-Saint-Merri headquarters, it continued to sell—wholesale—pounds of its small range of excellent teas to exclusive French clients, as it had done for the past hundred years. There was no retail business, and it never would have occurred to Marthe Cottin to have her cus-

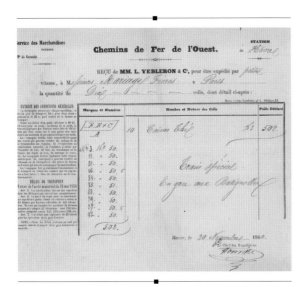

tomers sample her products on the premises. In fact, nothing had changed since the nineteenth century in the vast warehouse-and-office space, stacked with exotic chests, where some of the finest teas in the world were received, opened, tasted, and re-packaged. Neither the location nor the setting nor the methods—nothing had changed. Mademoiselle Cottin, a childless spinster, had been born in the building across the street, and was now in her eighties. Like her father and grandfather, whose expertise she had inherited, Mademoiselle Cottin's running of the firm was based more on her great knowledge of tea than on her management skills. Her relatives were uninterested in the tea trade. So she worked alone, assisted by a single employee, Marcelle, whose tasks included hand-stitching the cotton muslin used to make tea sachets. But Mademoiselle Cottin had one priceless asset—an

extraordinary address book rich with one hundred years of suppliers as well as clients. In China, India, and Ceylon, every producer of fine teas knew and respected the venerable Mariage firm. Mademoiselle Cottin didn't travel herself, but it was she who did the tasting and the buying. Quantities, costs, and profits didn't interest her—only quality counted. And her clients could rely on that.

She knew that this asset was a fragile one. She had no successor. On certain evenings, after a hard day's work, she would say that the business needed fresh blood, new energy. Without wanting to sell, she was seeking a person to whom she could transmit her expertise, who might expand the business and

maybe one day wind up running it. In 1982, she found two people—two young men who came from completely different horizons. That was the start of a bold venture and a wonderful tale.

The first young man was Richard Bueno, a thirty-year-old Dutchman. He had moved to Paris a few years earlier, and was working as a legal expert after having exercised several other professions. His mother was born in Bloemfontein, South Africa, while his father came from Paramaribo in Dutch Guyana (now Surinam). Bueno inherited his interest and taste in tea from his half-Indonesian maternal grandfather, who owned a tea estate in Indonesia. As a boy, Bueno had played rugby at international level, yet now he was a refined aesthete. And he was constantly on the go—ever since he left his native Holland at a young age, he traveled constantly. Yet he always kept his feet on the ground. He was an enterprising man of action, a hard worker who also had a good deal of intuition and a great sense of human relations. He was both a visionary and a realist. Then aged thirty, he was seeking a profession that would enable him to settle down

When newcomers Richard Bueno and Kitti Cha Sangmanee began exploring the world of tea, they greatly benefited from the family reputation: in China, India, and Ceylon, every producer of fine teas knew and respected the venerable Mariage firm.

even as he traveled the world. A business that would exploit his qualities and provide him with some kind of equilibrium.

One fine day in 1982 he heard that the owner of a tea importing firm, Mariage Frères, was seeking a successor. Tea? In France, the land of coffee? A land where tea was drunk only by rich old ladies who received guests at five o'clock with petits fours? As customers go, they were an endangered species. It would be madness to go down that dead-end route. On the other hand, thought Bueno, the tea trade also meant India, China, and distant voyages—all his grandfather's stories about the tea estate came flooding back. He decided it was worth a look before rejecting the idea. So he found himself wandering into the premises on Rue du Cloître-Saint-Merri, catching the scent of another world. There he met Marthe Cottin, and as the elderly spinster told him the long story of the Mariage family, he studied the chests of tea bearing exotic names, and he cast an eye at the list of glamorous customers. Obviously, there was no quick fortune to be made from this old, cluttered warehouse. The market for tea in France was too limited, especially when it came to high-quality teas. And yet the French were a nation of people with refined palates, with a sense of curiosity, with an open-minded attitude to novelty. It might just be a fascinating task to convince thousands of men and women of the exquisiteness of Mariage teas. Such ideas were at least worth thinking about, said Bueno to himself. But he hesitated. Before making a decision, he wanted some advice. He wanted the opinion of someone with whom he shared a taste for fine things and a poetic approach to life. That someone was his friend Kitti Cha Sangmanee.

Sangmanee was the second young man. Then twenty-eight years old, he came from a grand Thai family that had produced many talented men who served Thailand well. His father, a doctor, liked to relax by taking his children to the orchards he owned outside Bangkok. Kitti Cha's best subjects at school in Bangkok were the artistic ones, and he dreamed of pursuing an artistic career. But his parents wanted him to enter the diplomatic field, so he studied political science at college in Bangkok. In order to prepare for his future career, he left for France and enrolled at the Sorbonne where he wrote a dissertation on international maritime law. It was in Paris where Sangmanee met Bueno, and at the Sorbonne where

he became friends with Philippe Cohen-Tanugi, who would later become a key member of the management team at Mariage Frères.

Back in 1982, when Bueno asked him to have a look at the Cloître-Saint-Merri premises, Sangmanee was a serious student, all the more studious in that he had to work hard to improve his high-school-level French. His knowledge of tea was almost non-existent. Thailand produced very little of it, and as a child he drank only green tea. That was it. So, in turn, Sangmanee's foray into Mariage Frères was another trip into unknown territory. In fact, he recalls feeling a little like Howard Carter entering the sealed tomb of Tutankhamen for the first time—he was entering a space where time had come to a halt, where everything was preserved in its original state, where dormant treasures were crying out to be brought back to life. Sangmanee was perhaps even more amazed than Bueno. Here, just a stone's throw from the ultra-modern Pompidou Center with its light-drenched library where he studied regularly, was this age-old warehouse, stuck in the past, barely lit, its woodwork embalmed with age and smells. Here, among stacks of wooden chests and old-fashioned sifters, everything was still done by hand under the watchful eyes of the ancestral portraits on the walls, all governed by a marvelous old lady from another era. Sangmanee suddenly found himself in a quaint Europe that he thought had vanished forever. Yet here it was before his very eyes. Even before learning anything else, even without considering that tea was the main product here, Sangmanee fell madly in love with this timeless décor where there reigned, for a little while yet, a frail soul. To top it all, Marthe Cottin served him tea in a chipped cup. It was an orange pekoe from the Pettiagalla estate, served with sugar but no milk—for the first time, Sangmanee discovered the subtle savors of tea, something he would never forget. Carried away by the magic of the place, without further reflection, he advised his friend Richard to take the leap.

Bueno nevertheless took things one step at a time. He first joined Mariage Frères as a volunteer apprentice, taking the time to learn the basics of the trade and the ins-and-outs of the company itself. He also took his time before making a final decision. A pragmatist, he went over the books. Revenues were

tiny, the outlook uncertain. With every passing day, however, he became more aware of how underexploited were the firm's accumulated treasures, its long history, its sterling reputation, its contacts, its expertise. So he began to think about ways of exploiting and even enhancing them.

Sangmanee, meanwhile, was still under the shock of his first encounter. His regular visits to the nearby library gave him an excuse to look in on Bueno every morning. He began lingering at the Cloître-Saint-Merri premises longer and longer every day. The two friends were fast learners, thanks to lessons from the owner they affectionately called "Mademoiselle Mariage." Bueno focused on management and trade, while Sangmanee became fascinated by the art of tea. He discovered the extent to which the world of tea involved creativity, a creativity not unlike the fine arts. The beauty of tea leaves, the art of blending, of tasting, the aesthetics of tea services—everything delighted him, awakening unknown talents. He also discovered the subtle but distinct tastes that characterize teas of different origins, from the hint of berries in certain Indian teas, to the scent of chestnut in semi-oxydized teas from Formosa, to the smooth fullness of black China teas. A whole host of completely unexpected perspectives was suddenly opening up. In a matter of weeks, Sangmanee had put international law and diplomacy behind him forever. The two men's minds were soon made up. Bucking the advice of all their friends—who thought they had gone mad—Bueno and Sangmanee abandoned their respective careers and went to work full time at Mariage Frères in an attempt to expand the business in collaboration with Marthe Cottin. They worked fifteen hours a day for many months, without a penny in salary. The venture was fueled purely by passion.

In those days, tea barely existed as a beverage in France, as in most other European countries. Mariage Frères was one of the rare importers of high-quality teas. Meanwhile, the few tons of tea sold by supermarkets and coffee merchants were just a stale imitation of "English" teas or were cheap-flavored blends. In order to get a better of idea of tea-drinking habits in Europe, Sangmanee began to visit various countries, seeking out tearooms and specialized retailers. Then he explored England, the home of "tea time" where every inhabitant consumes five or six cups of tea per day. But what he found there sorely disappointed him: those six daily cups were always the same tea, rather poor quality tea at that. He discovered just how little was known about tea in England, the land that had set the tone for the drink, where it was an integral part of the lifestyle. It was primarily sold in the form of tea bags found in supermarkets.

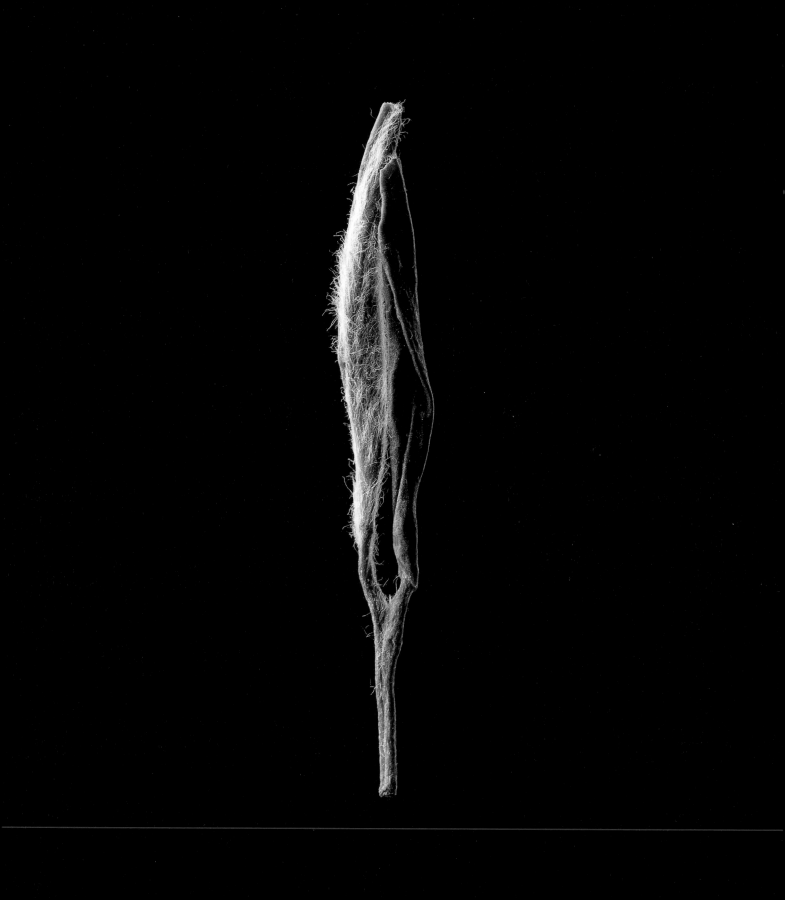

BELOW *Thé de la Bonne Étoile is a hand-crafted green tea from Hunan that develops a delicate hint of mandarin orange. Green teas are unoxidized, being immediately roasted or sweated.*

RIGHT *A leaf of Thai Beauty, an extraordinary variety of "blue"—or semi-oxidized—tea discovered in the Golden Triangle by Kitti Cha Sangmanee. Blue teas undergo an oxidation process that ranges from 12% to 70%, depending on the region of production—China, Formosa, Japan and, more recently, Darjeeling and Thailand.*

LEFT *Highly rare "white" teas acquired their name from the fine white down covering their silvery leaves, which are simply withered, then dried, to produce a crystalline liquor. Neige de Jade (Jade Snow), shown here, is plucked only at dawn on the Arya tea estate in Darjeeling. Each leaf is carefully wrapped in silk cloth and rolled by hand, yielding fragrances of young growth with overtones of white flowers.*

"When I entered the fragrant warehouse for the first time, something inexplicable happened, something wonderful and strange. I had the feeling I'd stepped into another era."

KITTI CHA SANGMANEE

Even in fancy hotels in London, where afternoon tea was a venerable institution, the list of teas was limited to five or six varieties. Sangmanee suddenly realized that the quality and variety of teas offered by Mariage Frères was far greater than anything found in Britain itself. And that was because the old French firm did not consider tea to be a common, ordinary beverage, but rather a refined, high-quality gourmet experience. In France, the land of gastronomy, Mariage Frères had quite naturally, if unknowingly, been selling "French-style tea." By preparing blends for its clients—teas that reflected taste at the Ritz and Ladurée—Mariage Frères was forging French tastes that suited France. In general, this meant sweet, light teas, never bitter, yet with a marked character that married well with certain gourmet foods. Therefore, reasoned Sangmanee, if Mariage Frères were to expand, it would be better to develop this idea of gourmet tea rather than trying to imitate the bulk strategies of English tea companies or simply appealing to more customers through clever advertising. Gourmet, French-style tea drinking could be encouraged by significantly increasing the range of teas on offer, by seeking out the best leaves and best harvests the world over, by inventing, if necessary, new terms for new teas. A born-and-bred Frenchman might never have had this brilliant idea of marketing tea the way fine wines are promoted. It probably required the insight of a foreigner new to France, dazzled by the broad range of gastronomic tradition in France, to perceive and promote French tea connoisseurship.

In 1982, "French teas" were still little more than an abstract notion. Nothing guaranteed that the idea would sell, because the two men had not yet verified one crucial condition, namely their actual ability to import a large number of outstanding teas into France. If they intended to offer a list of teas that could rival the list of wines flaunted by a great vintner, then they needed a broad range of excellent products. Not only did such a range not exist in France, but none of the tea-producing countries exported anything other than ordinary varieties. China was still a closed continent that exported just a limited selection of standardized tea—jasmine-scented green or black—reserving the best teas from its extraordinary estates for the Communist hierarchy. India exported only Darjeeling, making no distinction between harvests, yet at a

Yin Zhen "Silver Needles"
a white China tea

Yunnan d'Or
a black China tea

Gyokuro "Precious Dew"
a green Japan tea

Brumes d'Himalaya
"Himalayan Mist" a black
Darjeeling tea

Thai Beauty
a blue "semi-oxidized" tea

Pu-Erh d'Or
a matured China tea

Opium Hill
a blue Thai tea

Neige de Jade "Jade Snow"
a white Darjeeling tea

price that discouraged most consumers. Ceylon thought only of pushing its mass-produced teas—its great estates were almost completely unknown outside the island. As to Formosa with its Oolongs, and Japan with its Senchas and Matchas, they never dreamed that their exquisite teas could one day excite the taste-buds of more than just a handful of Western connoisseurs.

Therefore, the first thing the two young men had to do was to talk to brokers in tea-producing countries. Travel in China was still restricted, so it was in Hong Kong that the best China teas were to be found. There the name of Mariage Frères, known to several generations of tea brokers, opened many doors. In 1983 Bueno and Sangmanee were able to meet dealers who had never sold a single leaf of tea to Westerners. And the two men made their first marvelous discoveries of teas unknown in France: extremely select harvests of green tea, and also of whitish teas with silvery-white leaves, which had no name in French. Sangmanee dubbed it *thé blanc,* "white tea," just as he would invent other names in French in subsequent years to cover yellow teas, red teas, crafted teas, sculpted teas, matured teas, young teas, and so on. He also devised a system of French appellations, or categories, for teas: *grand, royal, impérial, d'argent* (silver), and *d'or* (gold). These terms, specific to French-style teas, were soon adopted by numerous competitors in France and thus became the accepted vocabulary not only in France but in other parts of the world. After the two men visited Hong Kong and made a fruitful incursion into Canton on mainland China, they took other trips to Japan, India, and Ceylon, where they met producers and brokers of high quality teas, all eager to export. At that point, Sangmanee began spending six months of every year traveling to tea-producing countries.

Thus the first condition for developing the realm of French tea connoisseurship had been established—it proved possible to import a hundred new varieties that were totally unknown in Europe. Of course, the extension of this realm required a second condition—these new, and more expensive, teas had to find buyers. Not only did such teas require a change in habits, not only did they call for an effort of discovery, but they cost significantly more. It soon became apparent that most retailers of Mariage Frères teas (specialized tea-and-coffee merchants, and even some glamorous establishments) were unwilling to take the leap. Mariage Frères still lacked a strong marketing image, because it had never sold teas under its own label. This time, it was Bueno, the visionary businessman, who had the bright idea: Mariage Frères would go retail,

selling teas under its own label not only in the warehouse on Rue du Cloître-Saint-Merri but also by mail-order. Just as a fine vintner organizes free tasting sessions, so Mariage Frères would propose, exceptionally, free samples of some outstanding teas. This idea appalled Marthe Cottin. "What? Customers rummaging among the tea chests right on these premises, only to buy 100 grams of a tea that they can sample at the counter? Madness." But Mademoiselle Mariage had acquired an almost maternal fondness for the two lads, and let them have their way. Sangmanee wrote the company's first retail catalogue, initially titled *Le Guide du Thé,* later changed to *L'Art du Thé,* and finally *L'Art Français du Thé*— "The French Art of Tea." The first version, published in 1984, offered 250 varieties of tea for sale, including one hundred teas—from some twenty countries—that Sangmanee had tasted and purchased himself. The quality and quantity of teas offered for retail represented a world first in the history of tea.

More and more people began wandering into the Mariage Frères premises. First it was just a few insiders, then word-of-mouth spread to connoisseurs, and soon sophisticated tea-lovers were heading for the place. Thanks to good coverage in the press, success was swift, and in no time ordinary people in search of new sensations and new gourmet experiences were dropping by. Success was initially social, before becoming financial. Every day, dozens of customers and curious individuals, generally young, would wander into these unique premises. They would fall under the spell of the old warehouse, where almost nothing had changed. They breathed the same fragrance, saw the office through its glass partition, sampled teas at the old blending counter, and gazed at the old chests, ancient containers, and old-fashioned brass scales. Marthe Cottin was always there behind the cash register, keeping an eye on her dominions. A warm and friendly atmosphere reigned on Rue du Cloître-Saint-Merri, so different from traditional tea salons in

RIGHT *The sky-lit tearoom on Rue du Bourg-Tibourg just before tea-time. Opened in 1986, one year after the retail store, the tearoom was designed in a "colonial" style that reflects the firm's tradition of putting a "French touch" to exotic taste sensations. On certain days, a thousand customers pass through these premises.*

Paris. Customers could learn to appreciate tea in new ways there. Almost all of the early pioneers are still customers and friends of Mariage Frères today. One of the most enthusiastic newcomers, then aged twenty-four, was Franck Desains, who would eventually play a key role in the firm, as will be recounted later.

As far as Cottin was concerned, a new chapter was beginning for Mariage Frères. A chapter that fulfilled her desire to see the company flourish once again, but a chapter that she felt should be written by younger hands. Those hands accepted her offer to sell the company, and she finally took a well-earned retirement at the age of eighty-two. Fortunately, the new owners were able to call on her for several more years, regularly soliciting advice from dear old Mademoiselle Mariage.

The friendly warehouse was steadily filling with a young, regular clientele, and everything was going for the best in the best of all possible worlds, when bad news suddenly hit. Marthe Cottin had never bought the physical building in which her company was lodged, and now the owner wanted the premises back. Despite a campaign mounted by the firm's loyal customers, who sent petitions to city hall, nothing could stay the sentence. Mariage Frères had to move. And it had to find premises worthy of the firm, of its spirit, of its history. A fine location was available on Rue La Boétie, right near chic Place de la Madeleine where there were already a number of specialist gourmet shops—an image that Mariage Frères could exploit. This option was seriously considered, but neither Bueno nor Sangmanee were enthusiastic about it. Just then they learned that a modest property on Rue Bourg-Tibourg, which they already rented as a warehouse, was up for sale. In 1984, Rue du Bourg-Tibourg was a nondescript street with little passing trade. The surrounding Marais district was still fairly derelict—the fashionable shops and lively cafés hadn't yet moved in. No other luxury-trade retailer, as Mariage Frères had become, would have had a moment's hesitation if forced to choose between fashionable Rue La Boétie and this unknown street in down-at-the-heels Paris. The two young owners obviously chose the latter. They chose it because it respected the Mariage family's roots in the Marais district, and because it corresponded much better to the warm and friendly setting that had lent so much charm to the company. The new owners did not want Mariage Frères to renounce its original identity or its history. On the contrary, the whole venture only made sense if they respected a tradition, enhancing and nourishing that tradition. Seen in this light, the decision to move to Rue du Bourg-Tibourg functioned as a kind of manifesto, a profession of faith—the Mariage Frères spirit would live on.

LEFT *The counter where tea is made.*
RIGHT *Two objects used in the Japanese tea ceremony: a bowl for powdered green Matcha tea, and the bamboo whisk (chasen) used to whip the tea in water. By organizing traditional tea ceremonies starting in 1985, Kitti Cha Sangmanee spurred the French to rediscover green teas.*

After much renovation work and much emotion on leaving Cloître Saint-Merri (the move was done with an old hand-cart that the original Mariage brothers had used to go to market), the tea house on Rue Bourg-Tibourg finally opened on August 1, 1985. Bueno convinced Sangmanee to create more than just a retail outlet. Within a year, the sales counter was joined by a tearoom that also served lunch. In premises that offered upstairs office space and were ultimately more suited to receiving customers even while retaining the original, friendly atmosphere, the two owners and their staff could comfortably develop and refine the concept of "French tea." An entirely new, French-style gourmet universe had to be built around tea. To begin with, that meant opening up to all the diversity in the world. Teas from everywhere on the planet, even the most unusual varieties, had to be offered to the budding circle of connoisseurs. The company's catalogue continued to grow, eventually numbering over six hundred teas, including some extraordinary harvests. The idea was not to impress people with astronomical prices, but to allow enthusiasts to indulge in a tea-fueled voyage to Sao Paulo, to dream of an Opium Hill in Thailand, or to savor the amazing magic of a yellow tea from China. In short, it meant giving everyone who wished a chance to discover the full diversity of the world of tea. Thus, right from 1986, when almost no one in France drank green Japan tea, Sangmanee organized the first festival of Japanese tea. For two years the company had been selling Sencha leaf tea, Matcha powdered tea, and a Genmaicha blend containing toasted rice and popped corn. But the first French customers to taste these Japan teas turned up their noses, finding them too much like spinach. Sangmanee thus realized that appreciating these teas required that they be presented in the broader context of Japanese culture. In 1985 already, he had organized traditional tea ceremonies at the Japanese Cultural Center in Paris. The following year, for his festival of green Japan teas, he organized tastings of eight teas, all in the sales catalogue, including a costly Gyokuro. These festivities—along with the marketing of the first cast-iron teapots based on traditional Japanese models, as made in Japan at the suggestion of Bueno—would steadily familiarize the French with these new savors, which eventually became rather fashionable.

"French-style tea" also implies a quest for the finest products used in blends and flavors, in the same way that great French chefs use the finest ingredients in their cuisine. One of the most striking examples of this quest is Mariage Frères' own Earl Grey blend—the company was the first to truly study

The Darjeeling region in northern India is home to eighty-seven grand estates on the slopes of the Himalayan foothills. Darjeeling teas are generally considered the most refined in the world—a distinction is often made between "First Flush" (or spring plucking), which yields a flowery liquor with a hint of green almonds, and "Second Flush" (summer plucking) with its flavor of muscatel and ripe fruit.

the countless nuances of bergamot and then to have exclusive essences composed at Grasse, the center of the French perfume trade. In this realm, French gastronomy's tradition of happily marrying flavors also comes into play—learning to take exotic ingredients and reinvent them in a French manner. At Mariage Frères, for example, Matcha tea, a green Japan tea in powdered form, is used to flavor vanilla ice-cream. The firm also makes a point of seeking out authentically grown teas, rooted in local soil and climate (like a vineyard), so unlike the anonymous, powdery stuff dumped into ordinary tea bags.

A magnificent demonstration of this insistence on authenticity was the company's "invention," in 1984, of seasonal Darjeelings. Up till then, British tea brokers held an almost exclusive monopoly on Darjeeling, imposing on the entire world their conception of a dark, black tea, thereby favoring the "second flush," or summer harvest of tea leaves. Sangmanee, during his travels to India, discovered not only the amazingly fresh and refined teas made from the "first flush," or spring plucking, with their notes of unripe fruit, but also noticed that tea estates in Darjeeling were often composed of different plots of varying quality. It took the company a certain amount of time and patience to teach its customers all the subtleties behind Darjeeling teas, and to get those customers to accept the difference in price they entailed. But this approach was so typical of French sensitivity to local, seasonal produce that now the arrival of the first spring batch of Darjeeling—the year's *thé nouveau*—as well as an appreciation of the summer and autumnal harvests throughout the year—has helped to shape the firm's pioneering image.

This variety of tastes and nuances, this concern for detail and subtle appreciation, couldn't fail to stimulate yet another French passion—discussing gourmet experiences in a language as precise as it is poetic. Mariage Frères invented an elegant, learned idiom for discussing tea in French, sometimes borrowed or literally translated from foreign terms, covering not only the origin of the leaf, it appearance and grade (something people never discussed before), but also its characteristic flavors and the best way to make it. This latter point—to be discussed in a subsequent chapter—was another major revolution triggered by

The sensual universe created by Mariage Frères
is based on subtle combinations of flavors,
fragrances, colors, and textures. Here the aroma
escaping from a Brûle-Parfum teapot harmonizes
with a cinnamon-wood sugar box and the velvety
richness of Chocolat des Mandarins.

Mariage Frères. For the first time, a tea merchant supplied a "user's guide" for each variety. Customers are free, of course, to add sugar to green tea, to add milk or lemon to a fine Darjeeling, or let Assam steep for half an hour—the world of tea is still a free one. But Mariage Frères points out to French customers that none of them would ever add sugar to a great bottle of Bordeaux, nor syrup to an excellent Champagne. For people who want to discover all the nuances of a tea that has been carefully grown, plucked, and hand-processed according to strict, age-old methods, it must be drunk in the appropriate manner. When this "appropriate manner" is respected in Mariage Frères' own tearoom, certain customers grow impatient; whereas ordinary tearooms will serve the beverage two minutes after the order is placed, some of Mariage Frères' fine teas require a quarter of an hour before they can be brought to the table.

Meanwhile, Kitti Cha Sangmanee and Richard Bueno steadily developed the Mariage Frères "look," refining it year after year. The original colonial image, simultaneously French and exotic, translated into a pale yellow logo against black ground, which became the firm's distinctive mark on bags and boxes. The use of black startled some people for whom the world of tea was always associated with red and gold. But the two friends trusted their instincts and soon proved, once again, to be visionaries; two or three years later, Japanese designers launched the rage for black in Paris fashion.

Franck Desains, hired by the company in 1987, actively participated in developing the Mariage Frères image. He had been recruited to work in a purely commercial role, but it was soon realized that his creative imagination was useful in many other fields such as the design and production of objects, packaging, scents, and even certain gourmet recipes. He soon therefore joined Sangmanee and Bueno's brainstorming factory, where work was more a question of self-fulfillment than sweatshop labor. After having unearthed a sewing machine to stitch the cotton muslin bags—Marcelle's nimble fingers having taken their retirement—Desains designed the little black box in which the tea bags would be sold. This timeless packaging is still used today for the twenty-four varieties of tea sold in muslin bags. In constant liaison with his two friends, he also designed new packaging for products made in traditional fashion by Mariage, although presented in new recipes and original forms—sweet biscuits, chocolate, and above all tea-flavored jelly. A keen connoisseur of fragrances, in 1989 Desains devised the first tea-scented candles, which will be discussed later. They revived an old Mariage tradition of manufacturing candles, but unlike

*A waiter descending the stairs of the shop
and tearoom on Rue du Faubourg-Saint-Honoré
in Paris, which opened in 1997. A haven of peace
and light near the busy Place de l'Étoile,
it is frequented by numerous celebrities.*

Aimé's efforts a century and a half earlier, these products met with phenomenal success. Like all the company's inventions, they were immediately copied by many imitators.

Two or three years after it opened, the Mariage Frères tea house on Rue du Bourg-Tibourg had already become a rallying point for every gourmet in Paris. And once it found its way into tourist guides, people from all over the world started pouring in. Much of the shop's success was due to the tea-based dishes served in the tearoom at lunch time, which constituted an original contribution to French cuisine. First, it was suggested that dishes be accompanied by specific teas, as would be done with wines, then, after a careful elaboration beginning with the introduction of tea-flavored pastries, an entire range of tea-based gourmet cuisine, including savory dishes, was developed. Innovation here concerned not only a new approach to French cuisine, but also a new approach to eating itself—long before French law required it, smoking was banned in the tearoom. Even more outrageous, as well as contrary to all commercial logic, Mariage Frères decided that coffee would not be served. It thus became the only restaurant in France where the little black beverage could not be ordered! However, the owners were determined not to sully the amazing fragrance of five hundred teas, impregnating the wooden walls with a sublime materialization of the Mariage Frères spirit.

While these innovations were not always easy to sell, Mariage Frères nevertheless enjoyed amazing success within a matter of years. The world of French tea that Kitti Cha Sangmanee and Richard Bueno had envisaged clearly met a real need, namely, the gourmet resurrection of the oldest beverage in the world. Over the years, this popularity led to the opening of four other tea houses in Paris and Tokyo, all respecting the letter and the spirit of the Mariage tradition. In Paris first of all, a second tea house opened on the Left Bank in 1990, at 13 Rue des Grands-Augustins; then another was inaugurated in 1997 at

PRECEDING PAGES AND BELOW *The Ginza salon is one of two Mariage Frères tearooms in Tokyo. It opened on October 16, 1997, an auspicious day because governed by a full moon. Present in Japan since 1990, Mariage Frères has become the ultimate reference in black teas, and is now the epitome of French savoir-faire.*

260 Rue du Faubourg Saint-Honoré, not far from the Arc de Triomphe. Meanwhile, the company had gained a foothold in Japan. A first tea house opened in Tokyo in 1990, followed by a true, five-floor tea house in the central Ginza district of the capital seven years later. In total, nine tearooms and shops were opened in Tokyo, Yokohama, Kobé, Kyoto, and Osaka. Mariage Frères became the absolute mark of reference when it came to black teas—the company's tea was even served on Japan Airline flights! For Mariage Frères was also viewed as a shining example of the French lifestyle in general: elegant, creative, romantic. The love affair between Japan and Mariage Frères partly rested on the way the company first absorbed authentic Japanese culture, only later passing it through a French filter to offer a happy blend of products to a Japanese public delighted with this marriage. These adaptations concern not only tea but utensils, as will be discussed later. In 2003, a second tea house opened on Meiji-Dori in the Shinjuku district of Tokyo. At the same time, news of the quality of Mariage Frères teas became known in Great Britain, the land of tea drinkers, and the company now has the pleasure of supplying some of London's elegant hotels, where afternoon tea is still a sacred ritual. The firm also holds the honor of supplying one of the most famous hotels in the world, the legendary Oriental in Bangkok.

In 1991, the upper story of the Mariage Frères tea house on Rue du Bourg-Tibourg was converted into a museum of fine, old objects related to tea and to the Mariage family. This museum was the brainchild of Bueno, who remained very attached to company history. Charged with the day-to-day running of the firm, taking part in every decision, constantly traveling, tasting every new harvest, this tireless traveler finally saw his life's project come to fruition. Ten years of sweat and enthusiasm had given Mariage Frères an international stature without sacrificing either its authenticity or its independence. Alongside Sangmanee, Bueno had pioneered all those things that now seem so obvious, that are now copied everywhere: the importation of the world's best teas, the drinking and appreciation of the finest harvests, French-style ways of blending and making teas, and tea-based cuisine. Then, in 1995, Bueno died after a terrible illness. But he left Kitti Cha Sangmanee and Franck Desains in charge of a company henceforth known throughout the world, employing over one hundred people and constantly seeking new ways of appreciating *Camellia sinensis*, as the tea plant is officially known. In honor of Bueno, Sangmanee composed a sublime blend, *La Route du Temps,* a "path of time" characterized by the lightness of green tea, the sweetness of flowers, the sharpness of spice. This blend pays fitting tribute not only to the spirit of the man, but also to the nature of the firm he created and set on the path to lasting success.

On looking back at everything accomplished by Mariage Frères since 1982, it is hard not to be impressed by the long road already traveled. The path began with a venerable firm that supplied a handful of excellent teas to a few exclusive retailers and led to an entirely new purveyor of extremely diverse colors, shapes, sensations, and feelings all based on one noble product—tea. A whole new world has been opened to all—everyone can admire the sights, savor the flavors, inhale the fragrances, enjoy this new realm of evolving pleasures. The men at Mariage Frères built a house that opened the door to an entirely new savoir-faire.

A WORLDWIDE
QUEST FOR TEA

I t is November in the far north of Laos, in what is called the "Golden Triangle." At this time of year, the mountainous region around Phôngsali is like a bad dream, haunted day and night by clouds and rain. The air is cold. On the road, which trucks have transformed into a muddy track ribbed with deep ruts, the travelers riding in a Japanese pickup are suddenly roused from their torpor at the sight of a lone woman looming in the mist. It is a Punoi woman—or perhaps Akha—in traditional indigo dress, barefoot, carrying a heavy wicker basket on her back. The nearest village is twelve miles away. Kitti Cha Sangmanee and Franck Desains are heading for the town of Phôngsali. They have been bouncing in the pickup for three days, since landing at the airport in Kunming, southern China. First they had to find the right border crossing, the one that permitted foreigners to enter Laos from China—an administrative detail that lengthened their mountain journey by several hundred miles. But the men are in no hurry. The date of their return remains open. Back in the Paris office of Mariage Frères, everyone knows that the two men are practically unreachable for six months of the year. And for several years now the two have been scouring the Golden Triangle—the kingdom of opium and wild tea plants—in search of the rarest of teas, the least known but perhaps the oldest varieties in the world.

This time, they're on the trail of a remarkable tea. They stumbled across it last year by chance, in a market in Luangphrabang, the former royal capital of Laos. The tea, tucked between stacks of fruit, ginger, and dried squirrels, took the form of a small cylinder of pressed leaves, tied with thin strips of bamboo. It gave off a subtle if distinctly smoky fragrance. Any other tea buyer in search of rare products would simply have made a deal with a merchant in Luangphrabang. But Sangmanee and Desains were not there just to buy tea at any cost. So they set off to find the tea, visit the plantation, meet the growers. Sometimes their long quests last several years before a deal is concluded—several years of tasting, comparison, conversation, and sometimes new creations. This time they've decided that they need to know more about this compressed tea, and therefore they are heading to the region where it is produced. In the market at Luangphrabang, they were told that it came from the north, from Phôngsali. And that apart from northern Laos it could be found only on a few markets in southern China. Phôngsali: the most remote province in Laos, a kind of spur jutting into China and Vietnam. It is the land not only of the Hmong people, many of whom live in Luangphrabang, but also the Phu Thai ("little men," strange Buddhists who do not cremate

their dead) and the Thai Khao (or "whites," so-called because of the color of the bodices the women wear).

The looping road seems endless in the thick mist. Every now and then, a large, wild tea tree can be glimpsed among the fruit trees. The travelers sense that somewhere ahead this gray haze must fill a steep mountain valley whose planted slopes each can see in his mind's eye. The Chinese driver, apparently in a hurry to reach their destination, drives much too fast along the edge of a cliff. He has already had a close call with a truck racing in the opposite direction, emerging suddenly from the fog. Fortunately, the ruts in the road slow the pickup, which suddenly sinks into a very deep one. Everyone has to get out and push, feet in the mud that is then sprayed by the spinning tires, splattering the travelers—there are days when customers back at Mariage Frères in Paris would have a hard time recognizing Sangmanee and Desains.

At any rate, as far as the two men are concerned, this trip to the northern tip of Laos, among peaceful peoples who grow the opium poppy only for medicinal purposes, is not the riskiest they have undertaken.

Other regions of the Golden Triangle are far more dangerous, notably the ones controlled by drug barons in Shan country in northern Burma (Myanmar). The two men have been exploring that area in recent years in order to bring back one of the finest green teas in the world, produced in the Ko Kant region, and totally unknown outside of Burma—apart from Mariage Frères. This tea has been hand-processed in the same way for millennia, in a wok, and evokes a universe of flowers and wilder notes of underbrush. It is a practically unattainable treasure, grown for local consumption among the poppy fields in a region outside control of the Burmese government in Rangoon. Ko Kant is no easy destination. Those who want to go there must be ready to risk their lives. Sangmanee and Desains were not yet aware of that fact when, in 1999, they first asked the Rangoon authorities for permission to enter the area. Authorization is required, because an official pass is mandatory. Once they had their pass in hand, the two men headed up through Mandalay and then traveled by car along the difficult mountain road to Lashio, where they reached a checkpoint. Beyond that point, the law of the land comes

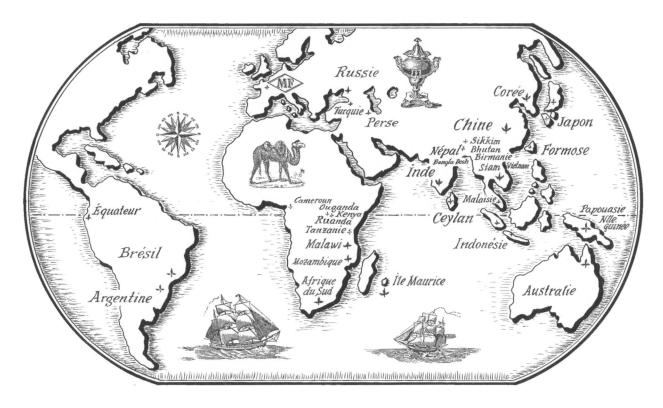

to an end, replaced by the law of the drug barons. Burmese soldiers do not normally allow foreigners beyond the checkpoint. But this Thai and Frenchman produced safe-conduct passes in proper order. A phone call to military superiors was nevertheless made, because the superiors may have had reasons—unbeknownst to the ministry in Rangoon—for preventing two foreigners from entering the area. So the travelers were told to wait. Hours passed. The soldiers seemed to have forgotten them. A good moment came to give the soldiers the slip, and so Sangmanee and Desains decided to sneak into the forbidden kingdom.

Just a few miles short of the Chinese border, the regional capital of Tashwe Htaw resembles a little Las Vegas perched on a tropical mountain at the ends of the earth—shady bars, casinos, and pharmacies jostle for space along the glamorous main street cluttered with lighted signs and piles of merchandise "made in Japan." The bars provide a pleasant way for locals to spend some of their dollars, the casinos satisfy the Chinese mania for gambling, and the pharmacies supply dope and the gear to inject it properly. Tashwe Htaw does not figure on any map—it is a secret drug-boom town, reserved for drug traffickers. But now the tea-seekers find themselves here. For several years they had heard talk of a tea produced in the area, but they had no idea how to go about finding it. Nor what kind of reception they would encounter.

On the first day, the reception was far from friendly. Soon after checking into a hotel, they were confronted by a group of heavily armed men in uniform. It was hard to know who these men were—Burmese soldiers, perhaps, or militia in the pay of a local drug lord. Or maybe both at once. Whatever the case, the men wanted to find out exactly what these two strangers were doing here. Tea merchants? That was a new one. Weren't they more likely to be American spies or, worse, journalists? A great deal of persuasion was required to calm the group of men—who were not completely convinced. For the entire rest of the journey, this group constantly escorted the two tea merchants, preventing them from entering certain zones or taking certain paths. All meetings were monitored. After a few days of investigation, Sangmanee and Desains managed to discover, snuggling in the mountain slopes, a few tiny, family-run tea estates that were particularly well cultivated. There was their treasure, right before their eyes, between the fields of poppy. The tea was ready to be plucked and then dried, in traditional fashion, in a wok. But first local contacts had to be made, the various gardens had to be compared, teas had to be sampled, and criteria of quality had to be established. Then a local agent had to be hired, and a return trip would have to be made. The name of Mariage Frères began circulate in these remote Burmese valleys on the Chinese border. The tea hunters have henceforth become known and respected.

The two men have had other adventures of this type, even in regions allegedly more peaceful. Take Darjeeling, for example. This apparently peaceful town in northern India not far from the border with Nepal and Sikkim, perched some 6,000 feet high at the foot of the Himalayas, is flanked by eighty-seven tea estates that produce some of the costliest black teas in the world, known for their extremely diverse and subtle flavors. Sangmanee has come here countless times since 1984, staying with planters who have become his friends. During a routine trip, which in theory would last just a few days, an extraordinary thing happened: the head of a local clan carried out a kind of putsch against the governor of this region, which enjoys a good deal of administrative autonomy. A mini civil war then broke out in Darjeeling. The airport was closed, trains were halted, roads blocked. Sangmanee and Desains would have willingly spent a few extra days, or even weeks, enjoying the charming view of the snowy peak of Kangchenjunga (where the Hindu god Shiva is said to reside), if bullets hadn't been whistling among the tea plants and if they hadn't had an important date back in Paris. But bullets were whistling and Paris was pressing, so their planter friends organized an escape in a four-wheel-drive vehicle that could leave the road, climb the hills, and follow the riverbeds. It took them three days of travel in the bush before they reached more peaceful regions of India.

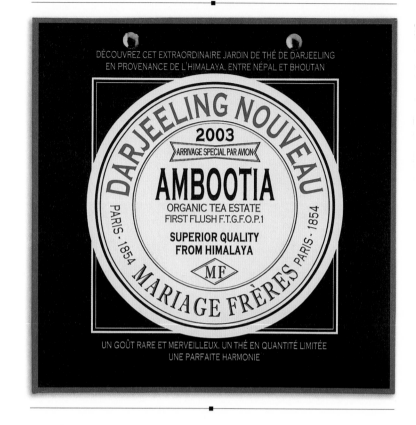

Darjeeling usually presents a more tranquil visage and more delightful adventures than this particular escapade. Mariage Frères plays an important role for these Himalayan estates, where the entire crop is exported. The French firm's presence on the market has encouraged planters to develop harvests on certain parts of their estates, secure in the knowledge that a buyer will be willing to pay a good price. They also know that, since the 1980s, Mariage Frères has acted as an engine that drives the market—its selections and innovations set the benchmark and stimulate increased demand for high quality teas that are more profitable for the estates. Two estates in particular now devote their best plots and their finest skills to Sangmanee's enterprise.

The first is the Ambootia plantation, where Sangmanee has been welcomed into the family home as a friend for many years now. Together, planter and merchant have conducted trials and tastings to develop a few highly select harvests, sold exclusively by Mariage Frères. In addition to Ambootia's prime black tea, plucked at specific times of the year—the first flush, harvested in spring, is characterized by a slightly spicy note while the second flush, plucked in summer, has a fruity taste with hints of black currant—the estate now produces three special teas: Brumes d'Himalaya (Himalayan Mists), Pivoine d'Himalaya (Himalaya Peony), and Fleur de Darjeeling (Darjeeling Flower). The two men spent years groping and experimenting, conducting botanical and agricultural research, to achieve these three masterful teas. Brumes d'Himalaya is one of the rarest and most expensive teas in the world. It owes its fabulous floral aroma with overtones of hazelnut and muscatel to the special plot of land on which it is planted, as well as to extraordinary methods of plucking and production. Like a white tea, it is composed

Laos

Laos produces fine green teas, grown mostly in the far north (within the Golden Triangle) or on the Bolaven plateau to the south. For centuries now, mountain villagers in the north have been making "bamboo tea," which is pressed into a bamboo-shaft mold and then shipped to markets in Laos and southern China. In Bolaven (where coffee is also grown), tea planters are often of Vietnamese stock, and still wear Vietnam's traditional cone-like hat.

Burma

Tea is an everyday treat in Burma. Men and women of all ages meet in the countless tea houses found in every town and village. The Burmese mainly drink green tea grown in the Shan states. Plantations are often tiny family gardens, where tea is processed by hand using age-old traditions before being sent to market. Burma has also retained its ancient tradition of lacquerware, and certain items such as tea bowls and containers are made of woven bamboo or horsehair coated with several layers of lacquer.

Thailand

Thailand—the home of Kitti Cha Sangmanee, seen here with a woman plucking tea—boasts wonderful blue (or semi-oxidized) teas found in the Golden Triangle to the north, grown by the Akha, Lisu, and Mien peoples. In the planters' workshops, tastings are conducted for leaves from each plot of land to choose the ones selected for Mariage Frères. In towns, tea merchants also sell —cha tjin— used for a light, cold beverage called "scented water."

RIGHT A basket of freshly plucked tea leaves in the Golden Triangle.

Laos

Burma

Thailand

exclusively of silvery buds, and plucking occurs only in the coolness of the evening; a delicate withering takes place overnight, then the buds are carefully rolled at dawn, having already been wrapped in a larger leaf for protection. Pivoine d'Himalaya and Fleur de Darjeeling also illustrate the difference Sangmanee's experience can make to a planter committed to his trade: when knowledge of the diversity of teas in the world meets ancestral know-how, entirely new teas can emerge, reviving old traditions even as they open new doors. Pivoine d'Himalaya, for example, is a tea unlike any other produced in Darjeeling. It is a white tea, plucked and produced according to the Chinese methods used in Fujian, thereby revealing overtones of green almond typical of first-flush Darjeelings along with the wildflower scent of white China teas. Fleur de Darjeeling stems from a similar mixed heritage, since this Darjeeling is semi-oxidized in the manner of Formose Oolongs, thereby yielding a totally original liquor enhanced by the amazing, honey-like sweetness of the addition of flowers from the *Camellia sinensis* plant.

The Arya plantation is another Darjeeling estate that demonstrates the value of trust and collaboration between a planter and Mariage Frères. The tea garden, perched on a steep slope reached by a road as spectacular as it is dangerous, has one surprising particularity: during the autumn harvest, one of the plots on the estate produces a tea with a scent of rose markedly more intense than any other Darjeeling. The first time Sangmanee tasted it, the rose aroma was so stunning that he suspected the planter of unscrupulously adding a little essence of rose, especially since the fragrance was already apparent in the dry leaves, even before it blossomed fully during steeping. After having verified on the spot that no subterfuge was involved, that the scent indeed sprang from the magic combination of soil and climate on that particular plot, Sangmanee bought the entire harvest—henceforth known to Mariage Frères customers as Rose d'Himalaya. The following year, however, the harvest produced a tea that was slightly less fragrant. Sangmanee therefore decided to encourage the planter to set about reinforcing, once and for all, the natural rose scent in the tea. The encouragement simply took the form of telling the planter that if he spent whatever time required, hired whatever technicians needed, and conducted whatever tests necessary to slightly modify a few steps in growing and processing, then Mariage Frères would buy the tea at a price that such efforts merited. By the very next year the estate produced a magnificent Rose d'Himalaya, the smoothest and most flowery of all Darjeelings.

Night has fallen on the road to Phôngsali, in deepest Laos, and the men seeking a tea unknown to the rest of the world are still far from their destination. The mist has been joined by darkness, making the road even more dangerous. The poorly adjusted headlights of oncoming trucks blind the driver of the pickup, yet he still fails to slow his breakneck speed. The minds of Sangmanee and Desains are elsewhere. As usual when they set out on a hunt, they muse about finding a treasure. The compressed, smoky tea they are sure they'll find—assuming they reach their destination—is one such treasure, but they already know it exists. More enticing is the dream of an unknown treasure. Maybe in this unexplored region they will stumble across some brand-new discovery, like Arya's rose-scented Darjeeling or like another miraculous tea unearthed in the Golden Triangle back in 1995. When Sangmanee tasted it for the first time, that tea triggered the second emotional shock of his life, after the one produced by his first encounter with Mariage Frères. He readily admits that part of the shock was due to the origin of this tea, his native land of Thailand. He had already been offering decent Thai teas to Mariage Frères customers for over ten years, but he knew that their main appeal was that they came from Thailand. This time, in his own country, in a region where only opium poppies grew, he discovered an extraordinary variety of tea. It was 30 percent oxidized and yielded a supernatural combination of aromas and flavors that included magnolia, litchi, and white peach. Sangmanee would call it Thai Beauty. It was exceptionally long in the mouth and produced a highly original, intense pleasure. As always, Sangmanee wanted to find the exact spot where this tea was grown, namely a small plot on the estate.

At that time, he was discovering all the nuances of teas on Thailand's side of the Golden Triangle. The area is marked by great ethnic diversity—families of Chinese stock from Yunnan, descendants of members

of the Kuomingtang army, and various minorities such as the Lisu and Akha peoples. Different varieties of tea are therefore grown in countless ways in a multitude of tiny estates hidden in the many folds of the hilly terrain. It took Sangmanee several years to distinguish and understand this variety, to compare methods and seasonal pluckings, to learn which planters were concerned only with profitability and which were respectful of tradition and interested in quality, ready to produce a first-class tea. This latter was the case, fortunately, with the planter who produced Thai Beauty. As soon as he tasted it, Sangmanee purchased the entire forthcoming harvest from that plot of land. Some months later, roughly one hundred kilograms of tea arrived at the Mariage Frères warehouse in Paris. Only ten percent of the tea, however, displayed the same characteristics and the same outstanding quality of the tea tasted back in Thailand. That portion was sold by Mariage Frères as a "seasonal tea" and was highly appreciated. But Sangmanee had to return to Thailand to discover why most of the batch fell below the required standards. He and the planter went to work together and finally, after several years of experimentation, developed a "made-to-order" product for Mariage Frères. Work was carried out not only in the field, but also in the office-cum-lab in Paris, because a tea so subtle and fine will not necessarily taste the same in a Western city as it does in the mountains of Thailand. Regardless of the condition of the tea leaves at the moment of crating, at one point or another they will be exposed to variations in temperature, humidity, and light, which may alter their qualities. The planter had to be informed of these reactions in order to incorporate them into his trials and methods. Meanwhile, when an exceptional harvest is discovered and acquired, it is placed under observation at Mariage Frères for several months before being put on sale, in order to learn how it changes over time. Some teas, such as Thai Beauty, actually get better down through

LEFT *These matured leaves are used to make mieng, a chewable tea highly appreciated in the Golden Triangle. Held by a strip of bamboo, they will be steamed for ninety minutes then packed in banana leaves and stored in a dark, airless place for a month.*

the years, like fine wines. Sangmanee likes to let them age, following the evolution of their aroma by tasting them at regular intervals. Unfortunately, this is a pleasure that cannot be shared by his customers, since European legislation stipulates that teas should be consumed within two years.

In the end, it took five years before Thai Beauty earned an entry in the Mariage Frères catalogue. In the year 2000 it was featured during the "festival of new teas," at which point customers could finally sample it. Every year since, the company has pre-purchased the entire harvest of this "made-to-measure" tea—which only comes to fifty kilograms! All too often, transactions between the French firm and great tea estates take place on this tiny scale. By way of comparison, just to underscore the difference between Mariage Frères and industrial manufacturers, pre-purchase contracts in regions of industrial tea production run into hundreds of thousands of tons.

The gratifying story of Thai Beauty was a cause for satisfaction not only among recent converts to these fine Thai teas, sold only by Mariage Frères. It also had a fortunate impact in Thailand, particularly when combined with other developments such as the marketing of Opium Hill, another excellent Thai tea discovered around the same time and the object of the same lengthy care. In a country that had been unaware of the extraordinary quality of some of its own teas—to such an extent that most of them were marketed throughout the world, including Bangkok itself, as "China" teas—this revelation profoundly changed the planters' attitude. In the Golden Triangle, where the Thai government is attempting to promote crops to replace the opium poppy, the possibility of producing teas with high added value has encouraged producers to plant tea, something the entire region can be proud of. Indeed, one fine day Thailand's princess royal, Maha Chakri, toured some of the plantations with Denmark's Queen Margrethe; a planter approached the queen with great respect and offered her a packet of tea, pointing out that she could drink it with confidence, since it was sold at Mariage Frères in Paris.

The notorious Golden Triangle, which covers the heaviest opium-producing—and therefore most secret—sectors of Thailand, Burma, and Laos, is in fact a "quadrangle." Only sensitive diplomatic considerations have silenced the inclusion of areas of southern China bordering the other three countries. The southern edge of Yunnan province, through which the Mekong River flows, is also an opium-producing region. How could it be otherwise? At the junction of all these countries, the climate, landscape, and peoples

India

PAGES 82-83

Plucking and processing tea is
still done in an artisanal way on
Darjeeling's grand estates, for that is
the only way to maintain the quality
of the finest harvests. Here Franck
Desains is seen with an estate's
technicians. After plucking, leaves
are sent to the weighing room, then
undergo various stages of processing,
which include oxydation
and the tasting of different batches.

Yunnan

PAGES 84-85

Plantations in Yunnan are known
for excellent black teas such as
Aiguilles d'Or, composed exclusively
of tender buds. Unlike green teas,
black teas undergo an oxidation
process, first employed in 14th-century
China during the Ming dynasty.
They are produced in the form
of whole leaf (Orange Pekoe),
broken leaf (Broken Orange Pekoe),
or tiny particles known as Fannings.

RIGHT *In Darjeeling, a cup of leaves ready for tasting.*

India

Yunnan

Compressed teas have been made for centuries in the Chinese regions of Guan Xi, Hu Bei, Szechwan, and Yunnan. Leaves of green, black, blue, and flavored teas are pressed into molds of various shapes (a brick, a bird's nest, or—in the Golden Triangle—a shaft of bamboo).

are the same—and the borders uncontrollable. On the road to Phôngsali, the strong odors of damp earth filling the night air are exactly the same as those encountered in China, the main region that produces Pu-Erh teas, a type of matured tea often pressed into bricks, one of the wonders of the world of tea. But that is hardly surprising, for the region is only fifty miles from Phôngsali, as the crow flies.

For Mariage Frères, the Pu-Erh saga began back in 1983, when Sangmanee and Bueno first tasted these teas in Hong Kong, along with white teas. No other merchants, apart from the Chinese themselves, had ever sought such tea. At that time, China was still largely off-limits to foreigners, and most of its tea-producing regions were hermetically sealed. So for many years Mariage Frères had to buy these strange Pu-Erh teas, along with fine harvests of white teas, in Hong Kong, without actually visiting the place of production or even, in the case of Pu-Erh, understanding exactly how they were made. The reason for the red color of these large leaves remained a mystery, as did the origin of the somewhat mossy flavor with a sweet, round, floral taste that countered the bitterness of tannin. It took a lucky turn of events, in 1997, to get to the bottom of these mysteries. Since the early 1990s, Sangmanee and Desains had been able to explore most regions of China. Countless times they had tried to free themselves from guides and government bureaus where standardized teas were brokered—they were fed up with the heaps of poor quality tea that stretched as far as the eye could see, specially designed to go into little bags for the greater profit of multinational corporations. In contrast, they had been excited by the many youthful peasants who spoke of tea with a glimmer in their eyes, who showed them two or three private tea bushes in the family garden, lovingly cultivated according to age-old techniques. Such bushes yielded exquisite teas. Sangmanee and Desains steadily built up surprising contacts, forged solid friendships, and learned to appreciate the profundity and poetry of the Chinese soul (ever ready to burst through the Communist veneer). Every time Sangmanee, a tee-totaler, found himself in a large cooperative where he was obliged to drink a cup of rice wine as sign of friendship—often by clinking bowls with hundreds of people filing by—he swore that he would

never again set foot in anything other than a village cooperative with no more than three or four workers.

The two tea hunters tend to prefer the province of Yunnan, for that is not only where the greatest variety is to be found, but also where small, wonderful estates and marvelous teas still exist. In addition to exceptional localized harvests, Sangmanee and Desains can buy very fine green and black teas, with supple, warm overtones, that are perfect for the company's numerous blends, including the now-famous "king" of Earl Greys, dubbed Le Roi des Earl Grey. So they return to Yunnan every year, and every year some little surprise awaits them. One day in 2001, for example, they were welcomed into a tiny town in Yunnan by the local Communist Party leader, who invited them to dinner. The dinner was not held in the official's home, but in a Buddhist monastery. And there, before partaking of the meal, the party official entered the temple and knelt to pray! It was also in Yunnan that Sangmanee and Desains were taken to see "the oldest cultivated tea plant in the world," one that is allegedly 3,200 years old and is still being

BELOW *Yiwu, a town in the Chinese province of Yunnan near the border with Laos and Burma, is the start of a road once taken by caravans of tea headed for the big cities of the north. The lengthy route allowed the tea to undergo a special maturation process, now reproduced in cellars, thereby creating Pu-Erh, a "matured tea" that is unique in being the only tea to improve with age.*

lovingly pruned. Finally, Yunnan is home to the mountainous zone that produces Pu-Erh teas, where wild elephants sometimes devastate tea estates—and poppy crops.

Everywhere in China, each tea plantation has its "elder" who is entrusted with the secret of local production methods. One day he will reveal the secret to his son or to a younger foreman. Usually, the "secret" is an

RIGHT *Pu-Erh teas are pressed into loaves, then wrapped in natural packaging in groups of five. Compressed teas have been produced for centuries in the Chinese provinces of Guangxi, Hu Bei, Szechwan, and Yunnan. Whether made from matured, green, black, blue, or flavored teas, they are pressed into molds of various shapes.*

open one, a fairly common way of plucking the leaves or processing the tea. In the hilly Pu-Erh region, however, where the delicious but strangely red tea is produced, the secret is a real one. As soon as they were able to enter the area, Sangmanee and Desains attempted to uncover it. Not only out of curiosity, but in order to be able to influence local methods, as they had done in Darjeeling, Thailand, and Burma. In order to produce a Pu-Erh of even finer quality, or one more adapted to French taste, or even—in yet another of Sangmanee's wild ideas that would certainly create another scandal—in order to marry it to bergamot so as to produce a truly amazing Earl Grey.

The name Pu-Erh comes from the town of the same name, some 6,000 feet high, the main market for tea grown in the Xishuanbanna region. But it was somewhat further south, in Yiwu, a town near the borders of Laos and Burma, that part of the secret was revealed. Yiwu is a trading center that was once the point of departure for mules transporting green Yunnan teas to Beijing, Guangzhou (Canton), or other major cities of the Middle Empire. Sangmanee and Desains had the good luck there to meet a local fan of Pu-Erh teas. He took them to the outskirts of town, showing them the paved road formerly taken, for centuries on end, by caravans of tea setting out on their long voyage. And he explained the phenomenon that occurred in those days: the green tea, shaped into flat loaves and wrapped in bamboo leaves, then strung together in packets of five, was placed in bamboo baskets, where it spent several months on the backs of mules before arriving in Beijing or Guangzhou. Scaling high passes, following misty rivers, crossing dry plains, subject to hot winds and driving rains, the tea was considerably altered during the trip. Although the local Pu-Erh specialist did not know exactly why, he said that sometime in the eighteenth century, or perhaps earlier, planters in Xishuanbanna decided to imitate the effects of this long voyage, during which the leaves matured, in cellars right in their own estates. Perhaps the increase in travel and trade sparked a local demand for such teas. Or perhaps new routes shortened travel time to the point of inhibiting the maturation process. The reason remains mysterious.

Whatever the case, our two tea-seekers had discovered the first part of the secret—Pu-Erh was not a specific variety of tea, but was originally a green tea that had undergone an aging process different from the standard oxidation effect that normally transforms green teas into black. The Mariage Frères men obviously wanted to know more about the exact nature of this special maturation process, but their Chinese friend kept his lips sealed, and answered only with an enigmatic smile. Sangmanee and Desains nevertheless spent hours with him discussing Pu-Erh teas, tasting an entire range of varieties. That is how they learnt that Chinese connoisseurs appreciate Pu-Erhs that have aged for several years—each from a specific vintage year, like fine wines—because such teas possess an incomparable finesse that lasts long in the mouth. This long aging process was reserved for leaves of the finest quality.

Increasingly eager to uncover more of the secret, Sangmanee and Desains visited dozens of Pu-Erh plantations. Every time, they were shown the tea bushes and invited to taste some remarkable teas. But when they asked to see the various buildings used to process the tea, they were invariably guided by their kind hosts to the warehouse where the tea was already packaged. And that was all. One day, however, they chanced upon a tea estate while the owner was away. They introduced themselves to the employees, ingratiated themselves with a few phrases in Chinese, and then asked to see around the place, in all innocence. And that is how they were led to a cellar where they discovered the real secret of Pu-Erh. They realized that the leaves were first compressed, under steam, into flat loaves that were then stacked and stored for several months under carefully controlled conditions of temperature and humidity. Several days later, the two men made another lucky encounter. This time it was a young Chinese tea expert who had just written an academic dissertation on the legendary Pu-Erh teas. He was able to provide specific details on the maturing process. On returning to the original estate, they presented their case to the planter who, realizing that he had nothing to hide any longer, agreed to work with them. The following year, after many weeks of collaborative effort, Pu-Erhs devised specially for Mariage Frères arrived in Paris. The company could thus add these exceptional teas to its catalogue—including one non-compressed variety, Pu-Erh d'Or—along with some very old vintage Pu-Erhs for connoisseurs back in Europe.

The nocturnal odors of the Chinese landscape dissipate along with the mist and the visions once the pickup truck finally enters a town with steep, poorly lit streets. Phôngsali, at last. After a few hours' sleep

in a freezing hotel room, Sangmanee and Desains explore this mountain village, split by the main road, perched some 5,000 feet high. Its alleys are paved with old stones and the traditional houses are made of wood or mud-and-wattle. Clouds hang low. And of course it is raining. From the heights of Mount Phou Fa, hovering over the village, they can see the magnificent mountain scenery that stretches endlessly beneath the clouds. On all sides, steep slopes host small terraced fields. Narrow paths snake among these tiny plantations. Once back in the village, the travelers begin seeking information. Soon a Punoi guide offers to lead them into surrounding areas in search of the peasants who produce the best teas. But where should they start? In these steep tropical hills, thousands of peasants grow crops on small plots of land and everyone owns a few tea bushes. The tea hunters spend several days exploring the area, visiting villages, meeting peasants. They are immediately struck by the extreme care that peasants take with the tea plants, scattered here and there among fruit trees and patches of bamboo

and sugar cane. It is the period of the final plucking before winter, and women wearing the traditional long skirts woven in colored stripes, their black blouses adorned with silver jewelry, delicately pick the leaves. Once their wicker basket is full, they go to empty it in front of the house, raised on piles. Inside, the leaves plucked the previous day are being sorted and prepared. Nothing seems to have changed for centuries. There are no items of plastic, no Western furniture, no electricity. The tea made in the dim houses, the one our travelers tasted in Luangphrabang a year earlier, has been perfuming these mountains since the dawn of time.

And although processing methods here follow all standard steps for green tea, the physical gestures, methods, tools, and odors seem to come from another era. The peasants seem to understand that they possess skills all the more precious for being timeless. The leaves are first withered on a bamboo rack hung above a hearth where a few logs slowly smolder. That is what gives the tea its characteristic smoky flavor. Once sufficiently softened, the leaves are rolled by hand, then heated in a wok. Next they are placed in small wicker baskets and are given a steam bath, in order to rehydrate them, which is crucial to the next stage—compression. Only when slightly damp are the leaves pressed into their mold, made from a shoot of bamboo. They remain in the bamboo mold for a while, which adds another note to their aroma. Once cooled, they can be removed from the mold, creating the form of a small roll of compressed green tea. To prevent it from falling apart, the roll is carefully bound with slim straps of bamboo. Then it is set aside to dry. This is the form in which the tea makes its way to markets in Laos and Yunnan.

Kitti Cha Sangmanee and Franck Desains thus visit a dozen small family farms, receiving a warm welcome everywhere. The producers of "bamboo tea" are proud that foreigners are finally showing an interest in the tradition they have proudly maintained for generations. Tastings follow one another, contacts are made and initial relationships nurtured. On leaving the area, bearing not only a few kilograms of tea but also new friendships, the two travelers know that they will be able to present the world with a new tea. Yet work still has to be done to reveal all its charms, and perhaps it will be elaborated in a special Mariage Frères way. The path might be long, but the men are in no hurry. By the time the pickup pulls out of Phôngsali for the endless return journey, the tea-hunters are already wondering when they will find themselves here once again.

Indonesia

PAGES 96-97

These pictures of Indonesian tea estates date from the early 1980s, when Richard Bueno (seen here in two photos) and Kitti Cha Sangmanee traveled in search of fine teas unknown in the West. Indonesia does not produce exceptional teas, but Bueno was delighted to discover the land where his maternal grandfather had grown tea. The colonial opulence of the planter's residence recalls the former importance of the tea trade in Indonesia. Today certain planters on Java and Sumatra continue to respect traditional methods, producing excellent black teas.

Vietnam

PAGES 98-99

Junks ply the waters in Along Bay, one of the most beautiful settings in the world, recalling how tea was once transported across the seas. Vietnam still offers several black, green, and blue teas of great quality, some of which are grown in the area of Thai Nguyen. Processing is still done in an artisanal way that hasn't changed since the appearance of the first French planters in the early 19th century. Pitchforks, often of bamboo, are used to air the leaves. Between visits to tea estates, Kitti Cha Sangmanee—ever in quest of new flavors—explores the shelves of spice and herb dealers.

Japan

PAGES 100-101

Some plantations in Japan, a land that developed a highly codified tea ceremony, seem to be laid out like a Zen garden. Also pictured here: a millstone used to grind green leaves into powdered Matcha tea; a young shoot of Gyokuro tea, the most sought-after green tea in the world; and the temple of Ankokuzan Shofuku-ji in Fukuoka, the oldest Zen temple in Japan, founded in the 12th century by Buddhist monk Eisai, who studied Zen in China and took it back to Japan—along with tea.

RIGHT The wonderful landscape shaped by rice paddies and tea bushes on the island of Kyushu in Japan.

Indonesia

Vietnam

Japan

3

ARTFUL COMPOSITIONS

F rom the scent of ripe fruit associated with the Bouddha Bleu blend to the subtle spices in sunny Mandalay to the honeyed fragrance of Pleine Lune, Kitti Cha Sangmanee has composed hundreds of special teas, both "classic blends" (of various kinds of leaves) and "flavored teas" (with additional fruit, flowers, spices, etc.). In his art of composition, everything begins with a specific taste—a virtual taste, one that arises spontaneously yet is associated with an experience, an idea, or another savor. Once he has mentally registered this taste, Sangmanee never forgets it. His amazing gustatory memory stores not only virtual tastes, but also the exact flavor of all the teas he samples—the leaves of a given harvest from such-and-such an estate in China or Darjeeling. Sangmanee himself still marvels at this strange phenomenon, a faculty that he slowly acquired but only fully recognized rather suddenly. It enables him, for example, to mentally conjure up the flavor of a tea tasted years beforehand. He calls it a "miracle," a kind of gift that he owes to Mariage Frères and that he feels is his most precious asset. Because once he had also learned exactly how certain flavors combine to create yet other flavors, his work began to resemble that of an artist who blends colors, almost automatically, to create just the right shade. When he adds a final flourish, apparently spontaneous like a magical brushstroke, it really reflects the culmination of years of experience, meditation, awareness, and practice. Working at a long table in his office where he often composes on Sundays, Sangmanee has long known, beyond all possible doubt, that to give body to a virtual taste he must, for instance, combine certain green teas with a specific flower from Thailand, or certain Oolongs, more or less oxidized, with a specific green almond. The new taste may trigger a strange alchemy or association, for example the hint of green almond in a first flush from a Darjeeling estate with a note of hazelnut in a certain Yunnan and the fresh grassiness in a given Sencha. For years now, he no longer hesitates, no longer needs to conduct preliminary tests, no longer even measures amounts precisely—a few pinches or a fistful will do. Only once the composition has been completed does he write everything down in grams and percentages, for practical reasons. Then it's all over. It may look like child's play, but the resulting taste opens the door to an entirely new universe.

This mastery is the result of a long process. The genesis of the creative act is more complex than it first appears. In fact, in order to understand how Sangmanee's art developed, it is easier to begin by listing

Tea drinking has always willingly reflected traces of human history. And the twenty-first century is now making its mark: flavors, aromas, colors, and textures gathered from gardens the world over are orchestrated according to French taste—light yet sparkling, rich yet delicate, refined yet authentic.

everything he *doesn't* do rather than describing what he does. To describe what he does, to translate his art into words, would probably require a poem. For in many ways his compositions could be viewed as poems, paintings, or musical scores—like all successful works of art, even before the ingredients are deployed, a Sangmanee composition is above all a blend of talent, inspiration, experience, and technique so perfectly mastered that everything remains invisible even as it operates.

Let us therefore start with the simplest point. The composer of Mariage Frères' teas is *not* a "blender." Among standard tea merchants, blenders are expert technicians who perform two main tasks. First of all, they combine different leaves to obtain a standard, predetermined taste that must in no way change from one year to the next, so that customers will drink exactly the same beverage at breakfast throughout their entire lifetimes. This routine task was once a noble art in the days when the quality of leaves varied and those variations had to be masked by altering doses or replacing one part of the blend. These days, manufacturers often induce growers to use certain methods that produce the same leaves year after year—making the blender's task easier. The task has lost further luster because manufacturers seek above all to create blends that will never startle any person or any tastebud on the planet. They seek the most impersonal taste imaginable. The blenders' task thus involves, in part, eliminating overly good leaves, ones too rich in taste, ones that just might, somewhere in the world, surprise someone's palate. Their second task is to reproduce, year after year, the same flavored blends. Along the same lines, they monitor the identical reproduction of the same bland Earl Grey, the same standard green tea with jasmine, the same strawberry-flavored tea that tastes more like a soft drink than tea, all the while paying close attention to the economic ingredients of such frivolities—poor-quality leaves and artificial flavors make it possible to produce these teas for the cost of soda pop while guaranteeing that no costs will vary during manufacture.

That is why Sangmanee is not a blender. In fact, he is just the opposite. But you will never hear him discuss these industrial practices, much less condemn them. Blenders are simply not part of his world. They do not do the same things he does, so he brings no judgment to bear on them. When Sangmanee talks tea, he talks about his own teas, or the teas he tastes on estates scattered around the globe, preferably far from the beaten path. And when he discusses his own work of composition, he claims no special merit, nor even utters the word "work." He does refer to a certain experience, but above all he evokes a kind of mysterious, inexplicable aptitude. And he conveys his serene but unshakable determination to create *new* tastes, not at the risk of startling tastebuds but in the *goal* of startling them. For Mariage Frères must awaken customers' palates, must at all costs prevent them from becoming accustomed to standard tastes. Only then will miracles happen. Sangmanee displays no desire to please others, but rather a determination to stimulate his own palate. When people tell him that one of his new blends will be impossible to sell, he is delighted. The opposite would worry him. He never creates a tea to meet a demand. Because he knows from experience—to his surprise and delight—that his compositions usually triumph sooner or later over the long course of time. Yet you will never hear him claim the status of true artist. That, however, is exactly what he is.

Like all true artists, Sangmanee wasn't made in a day. When he first came upon Mariage Frères, the company had already been specializing in exceptional blends for a good, long time. Its policy was to use only rigorously selected leaves as the basis of its teas. Some people even thought that the firm was named not after a family but after its penchant for *marrying* teas! Marthe Cottin continued to compose, at the company's long oak counter, special blends for hotels such as the Ritz and the George V, and for up-market caterers such as Faguais and Ladurée. In 1984, roughly half of the sixty-or-so blends sold by Mariage Frères were venerable old compositions. Among the most famous, created either by the Mariage brothers themselves or by Cottin, and still available from the company today, it is worth citing Sultane (a breakfast blend of fine Ceylon teas), Empereur Chen-Nung (a China tea with delicate, smoky flavor), Majesty (an English-style blend of Ceylon and smoky teas), Amateur (black and green teas lightly flavored with jasmine) and Tzar Alexandre (the firm's Russian blend). Sangmanee allowed himself to revamp Tzar Alexandre somewhat, and in fact his first job at Mariage Frères entailed bringing certain classic blends up to date, and giving others more evocative names—Sultane and Chen-Nung, for example, are names of his devising. He later invented the names for most of his own compositions, thereby eliciting criticism from so-called purists who feel that a tea should not be titled like a poem or a painting—but perhaps they don't realize that the Chinese themselves have been giving poetic names to their teas for thousands of years.

The assignment assumed by Sangmanee was the creation of flavored teas. Prior to his arrival, Mademoiselle Cottin sold only the classics: bergamot-flavored ("Earl Grey") and jasmine-flavored teas. Most of her clients, in fact, ignored what they considered to be pointless whimsy. But the firm's new owners deliberately decided to extend this range, for they felt it would appeal to a younger clientele and therefore guarantee the company's survival. As far as they were concerned, however, this was not just a matter of good management or shrewd marketing. First of all, Sangmanee, who was just starting out in the trade, sensed that he would find his true calling in the development of totally new flavors; and second, this creativity corresponded to their idea of a "French art" of tea, enhancing its appreciation in every possible form. Often these blends also fulfill the French tradition of gastronomical delight, which involves not only pleasing the palate but also the nose and the eye. Just as wines are appreciated not only in the mouth but also for their bouquet and color, so a flavored blend can be appreciated in three dimensions: its taste, its fragrance, and its color as nuanced by spices, fruit, or flowers.

Therefore, in 1984 Mariage Frères listed thirty new flavored teas. Long-time company customers raised their eyebrows, and did not welcome them with open arms. The best-selling flavored blend in the early years was Tropical, with a heady fragrance of tropical fruit that appealed to sun-worshipers. Yet little by little, some of these initial compositions gained ground, ultimately rising to the status of the company's overall best-sellers. Noël, for instance, composed in time to celebrate Christmas 1984, became a favorite fairly swiftly. It probably represented Sangmanee's first great creation—festive for the eye and nose as well as the palate, it contains zest of orange (a traditional Christmas fruit) as well as spices such as vanilla, cinnamon, and cloves. Its name was wonderfully appropriate, for it became a perfect Christmas gift. No one else had ever thought of creating a special blend for a particular holiday, and yet these days every single tea merchant now sells a Christmas blend of some sort. It is unlikely that a Westerner would have come up with this idea—Sangmanee had experienced his first Christmas not long before, and therefore his imagination was still stirred by the magic of Christmas festivities.

In the same way, it is perhaps unlikely that someone from Japan would have ever conceived the blend called Sakura, the Japanese word for "cherry blossom." This green Sencha tea, subtly flavored with cherry blossoms, dates from 1984, the same year as Noël. Sangmanee wanted to find a way to express the Japan

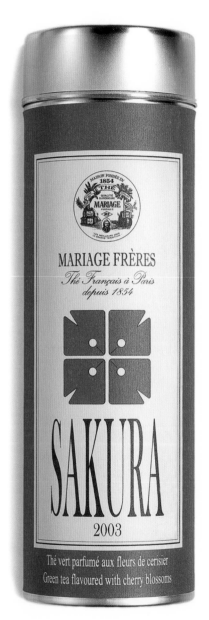

PRECEDING PAGES *Kitti Cha Sangmanee tasting several teas in his office-cum-lab in Paris. Experience, meditation, inspiration, and concentration are the ingredients of his creative method, designed to invent totally new flavors.*
FOLLOWING PAGES *A selection of classic blends and flavored teas.*

of his imagination. He never dreamed that in a matter of years this tea would become a smash hit in Japan itself. Mariage Frères first launched Sakura there on the very day that cherry trees blossomed, a day highly symbolic of spring and regeneration in Japan, eagerly awaited by all and celebrated with great festivity. Ever since, the company subtly nuances the tea's flavor each year and sells it on cherry-blossom day as a special holiday treat. Its great popularity in Japan can be partly explained by the delight the Japanese take whenever someone explores and inflects their culture. This pleasure harmoniously amplifies Mariage Frères' own determination to blend and combine cultures, without which the French art of tea would be meaningless.

Also invented in 1984, the world-famous Marco Polo blend only began to meet with success five or six years later. At present it has long held the rank of the firm's best-selling tea. Its personality (evoking distant lands), its silky roundness (the product of a complex association of exotic fruit and flowers), and its characteristic, immediately recognizable bouquet explain its great popularity. Sangmanee conceived Marco Polo as an imaginary voyage to China and Tibet, in the footsteps of great travelers of yore. This blend is typical of certain Sangmanee compositions that have become rarer with passing time and greater experience, namely teas born of a preconceived idea or the conscious intent to evoke a place or person, which means finding a precisely sought nuance. Teas of this type are often sentimental, and more recent examples, perhaps less easy to appreciate at first but admired by numerous enthusiasts, include La Route du Temps (the "Path of Time" mentioned above, dedicated to the memory of Richard Bueno and categorized as a "classic blend" rather than a "flavored tea" because it contains no added flavor apart from a hint of ginger). In this case Sangmanee was not trying to compose a simple green tea flavored with ginger (something already found in the firm's catalogue, for Mariage Frères also launched the rage for flavored green teas), but rather to create a new taste by combining ginger with other ingredients that would attenuate its strength, including a floral note of honey obtained without using honey. This new, unknown taste went beyond ginger. Based on a green tea associated with lightness, it reflected a desire to craft a tea that would evoke a mysterious voyage into the hereafter. Such ambitions are clearly a long way from those of a conventional blender.

In the same vein, it would never occur to a blender to compose a tea while reminiscing about his mother. Sangmanee has created two. Only one of them, Lune Rouge, is sold by Mariage Frères. This "Red Moon" is a feminine pendant to La Route du Temps, based on several green teas, a little ginger, and also various

Flavored teas represent a marriage of aromas. Black, white, green, and blue teas are usually scented with flowers (jasmine, rose, orchid or— as made famous by Earl Grey—bergamot) or sometimes with fruit, whether local or exotic. Flavored blends, meanwhile, are more inventive assemblages that skillfully combine a number of sensual fragrances.

types of rose petals. Here again, it was a question of concocting a totally new taste while thinking of a specific person, a taste evoking nothing less than that individual's personality. It is hard to think of a more personal creation. Some time later, tasting the other tea he had composed while thinking of his mother, he observed that it hadn't altered over the years and, more important, that it displayed something obvious he hadn't noticed earlier: the totally new taste that he had created seemed to be a natural flavor. On thinking about it, he realized that this was exactly what he had always been seeking—flavors that people might think were natural, that were present in nature in some part of the world or other.

Sangmanee's early teas were also marked by the bold invention of new Earl Greys, those classic teas flavored with bergamot. He began by studying bergamot itself, of which thousands of varieties exist (and which no blender had ever considered). He began ordering the rarest of bergamot essences—ones that suited his ideas—from Grasse, the town in southern France famous for making natural essences for perfume. The classic Mariage Frères Earl Grey, based on black tea, was soon joined, in 1984, by an amazing Smoky Earl Grey (made with a smoky China tea) and a magnificent Grand Earl Grey (made from a Ceylon with white tips). Continuing his research, he revolutionized the traditional concept of Earl Greys by creating lighter versions, combining a very subtle fragrance of bergamot with leaves of great finesse, yielding an Earl Grey Oolong (based on a blue Formosa tea) and an Earl Grey Impérial (from a first-flush Darjeeling). Because it married two highly refined ingredients, Earl Grey Impérial was an amazing success. In one fell swoop, Mariage Frères thereby invented the "Impérial" grade, which has subsequently been adopted by numerous other tea merchants, and also popularized first-flush Darjeelings. The company has gone on to extend the range of bergamot-flavored teas considerably, daring to base them on green China teas and to blend different leaves (an English Earl Grey made from China and Darjeeling teas). This range also includes a sublime Yunnan version (Roi des Earl Grey), an airy Sencha from Japan (Earl Grey Sencha), and a smooth, red matured tea (Earl Grey Pu-Erh). Mariage Frères' full palette of Early Grey teas, unique in the world, now includes some fifteen different varieties.

Thé des Poètes Solitaires

La Route du Temps
"The Path of Time"

Thé Céladon
"Celadon Tea"

Lune Rouge
"Red Moon"

Montagne de Jade
"Jade Mountain"

Esprit de Noël

Bouddha Bleu

Eros

This work on the endless nuances of Earl Greys, which he conducted throughout the 1980s alongside other investigations into jasmine and smoky teas, represented a crucial learning process for Sangmanee because it enabled him to discover how each basic tea would react in such combinations. At that point, he was able to attempt even bolder compositions, breaking with old routines at the risk of shocking certain connoisseurs. In 1986, for example, he was the first person to compose a tea comprising not only green and black leaves but also mint and bergamot. This "Casablanca" blend was a highly personal interpretation of Moroccan-style tea. The following year he innovated even more radically by combining, in a single blend known as Successeur, leaves of different grades, something no one had ever done before. In addition, Successeur felicitously married traces of two flavors thought to be incompatible, vanilla and smoked leaves. In this way, the cautious exploration of Sangmanee's early compositions, in which he would add a drop of bergamot or jasmine here or there, like a perfumer, or a gram of certain leaves to other leaves, steadily gave way to his current creative process as he learned and assimilated basic rules. This is the path followed by all artists who, once technical constraints have been fully interiorized, can give free rein to their inspiration and imagination.

Kitti Cha Sangmanee is not a blender, nor is he a Western-style, egocentric artist who loves to talk about his work and himself. Thus there is one dimension of his creative impulse that he never discusses, even though it can be inferred from certain brief allusions—namely, the spiritual dimension. It is fairly apparent that the thrust of his current creativity reflects an approach that is more than merely technical, indeed more than merely artistic. But all Sangmanee will admit is that he spends an hour a day in meditation. And that it frees him from demands, provides the vacation that he never takes, purifies him, gives him strength—and stimulates his creativity. Indeed, his art of composing teas closely resembles, in its principles and inspiration, the subtle Japanese art of flower arranging known as *ikebana*. This art is also a Buddhist ritual whose goals of simplicity and re-creation of natural beauty are therefore imbued with the Zen aim of attaining serenity. *Ikebana* is an art that attempts to express a mood in order to provoke that same mood in the beholder; an art, therefore, devoted to others, a generous art of sharing. And an art that always balances classicism with freedom. Furthermore, it is an art intimately linked to meditation and concentration. Finally, and above all, it is highly codified by a multitude of rules, yet once those rules have been learned the art harmoniously emerges from a single gesture that appears spontaneous.

The artist, however, still needs to have something to say, a feeling to share; the flowers still have to be selected and cut, the vase has to be chosen, as does the season. Behind all compositions completed in the flash of a single gesture there resides not just a spirit but also a process of gestation, a method. With Sangmanee—unlike, once again, blenders who seek a taste without knowing what they're looking for—everything *begins* with a taste. Or, more precisely, by two tastes. In general, things usually occur in the following fashion: one fine day, by chance—although often while traveling, because that is when his mind is most open and his taste-buds most alive—the taste of something he is eating will trigger another taste. In the same way that Marcel Proust's famous madeleine, dipped into a cup of tea, triggered his remembrances of things past and his sense of happiness, the taste of a Chinese or Indian dish, the flavor of a mushroom or hazelnut, the fragrance or zest of a piece of ripe fruit, or the scent of flower or spice can bring forth, almost by osmosis, another taste, a tea-related flavor that he will later try to re-create. Inspiration may also come from a simple savor or scent, or even an impression or the sound of a word. Although rarer these days, it might also come from a feeling for a loved one, or for a historical figure. All his senses are alert when, suddenly and mysteriously, a feeling gives rise to a new flavor experience. Sangmanee never sets off in search of a taste, it is the taste than composes itself within him.

And so the die is already cast: when he finds himself before his work table, months or even years later, at the moment when this imaginary taste is to be given form, his experience, skill, and concentration can complete the work in a matter of minutes. Sometimes, however, special constraints can guide the apparently straightforward process of composition. The idea of serenity or the silence of an evening, conducive to poetic creativity, can induce Sangmanee to compose, for instance, a mild tea suited to people who dread insomnia. The new taste is therefore the product of intersecting ideas; it will not necessarily be a tea free of theine, for without theine tea has no flavor, but a tea with little tannin and therefore no sharp tastes that will excite the taste buds and thereby awaken other senses. Thus was born Poètes Solitaires, a mellow blend of grand China and Darjeeling Oolong teas, perfect for a meditative, solitary poet.

"I've violated all the taboos.
I've blended white teas with green teas,
and green teas with black teas.
I've never composed a blend
with the idea that everyone had to like it.
Never. I compose for my own pleasure."

KITTI CHA SANGMANEE

Sangmanee's own taste has evolved. His compositions therefore reflect specific periods of his life, and sometimes he will later modify those teas. These days, he would not produce the teas he composed in the past. For example, he is less likely to use traditional black Ceylon varieties, to which he was highly attached at first, as the basis of his flavored teas. He now finds that those teas do not have the right hint of mystery. So he prefers the more intriguing, golden notes found in certain Assams and Yunnans. But only "certain" ones, namely those that don't exactly resemble what they're supposed to be. He will therefore blend them with other teas, for almost none of his compositions employ just one single tea. To keep things simple, the clerk behind the counter will say "Darjeeling with bergamot," but in fact that means several Darjeelings, without which the perfect note could never be struck.

Kitti Cha Sangmanee is now at the height of his art. And since he seems to want to go ever higher, ever further in the invention of new tastes, ironic commentators might now expect him to levitate. His mastery of the art of composition enables him to meet incredible challenges in the most natural of ways. These include obtaining the taste of a particular fruit or spice without actually using that fruit or spice; as already mentioned, the hint of honey in La Route du Temps is produced without honey. Similarly, to give just two other examples, the taste of citronella in the "Nile" blend of green teas called Thé sur le Nil is produced without citronella, as is the impression of litchi in Montagne de Jade. The reason behind this approach is neither the challenge itself nor a desire to amaze, but the fact that the aromas and flavors he sought could not be supplied by the fragrance experts in Grasse—the flavor Sangmanee composed, when he thought about it, seemed even more natural. It is as though his art now allows him to re-create natural flavors more surely than nature herself. This has led to true curiosities, such as the search for first-flush teas that do not display the usual characteristics of first flushes, or teas more wild than cultivated, such as certain green teas from Laos. Sangmanee's mastery also enables him to respond successfully to suggestions made by Franck Desains, who is increasingly involved in the conception of new teas. It was Desains who had the idea—visual in inspiration—of a magnificent "white and pink" tea in 2003. He felt that those two colors could be combined into a pure, airy harmony that would respond to a growing desire for serenity. According to Desains, white and pink are the colors of the future. He and Sangmanee therefore composed a blend, Blanc et Rose, based on one of the costliest teas in the world, a white China tea called Yin Zhen (Silver Needles), with the petals of rosebuds found in Morocco after long years of hunting. What, indeed, could be simpler or purer? At the same time, however, some people consider it scandalous to scent a white China tea with rosebuds (perhaps the same people who would never have heard of "white tea" without Mariage Frères). Jasmine might have been acceptable (as in Thé des Mandarins), since jasmine tea is a great Chinese classic. But not roses. The inventor accepts this criticism insofar as he himself would not have been so bold ten years ago. Nowadays, however, he listens only to his instincts. So to create such a wonderful tea, the two men sought the most subtle, most appropriately scented roses; then they chose, among the different kinds of Yin Zhen, the one tea that carried tiny hints of mandarin orange and truffles.

Sangmanee has now composed hundreds of new teas, both classic blends and flavored varieties. Not all of them are listed in the catalogue. Some have been discontinued, others are awaiting their moment. Sometimes no new blends will be presented in a given year. Indeed, Sangmanee may hold in reserve a certain number of compositions for very simple reasons. Mariage Frères' long-time customers, now initiated into the subtleties of grand teas, are wearying of certain flavors of berry, cinnamon, and orange, the very flavors that led them to discover the world of tea some twenty years ago; newer customers, meanwhile, now discover a range of blends sufficiently vast to keep their palates busy for years. And, on a more practical level, there is little room left in the tea houses for more varieties. Finally, Sangmanee composes fewer blends now than in the past—much of his creativity is now devoted to developing new harvests in collaboration with growers, as described in the previous chapter. This will not prevent dozens of new tastes from springing into his ever-alert mind between the moment that I write these lines and the moment that you read them. New tastes are perhaps the souls of wandering scents of paradise lost—having finally found refuge in Sangmanee's limitless memory they await, wisely and no doubt deliciously, for the day of their reincarnation.

MAKING FRENCH TEA 4

The people who make and serve tea in Mariage Frères' various tearooms all readily recount, with a smile, the dissatisfaction of certain first-time customers. The customer arrives, sits at a table, runs down the list of teas, and orders. Then waits. Ten minutes later, impatience mounts.

"Is my tea coming?" "It's on the way, sir," replies the waiter, "it's just being made now." When the waiter finally brings the tea a full five minutes later, the customer grumbles. "It takes you fifteen minutes to make a pot of tea?" The waiter silently pours the precious nectar into the cup. The customer automatically blows on the tea to cool it, then takes a tiny sip. Only to complain, "Hey, it's not even hot!"

And so it goes. Although less and less common now that Mariage Frères' advice on preparing tea has become more widely known, there are still a few customers who expect to be served a pot of boiling-hot water—in which a little teabag swims—in two minutes. Their discovery of French tea connoisseurship is therefore an unpleasant surprise. They haven't yet realized that certain teas must be steeped for a full fifteen minutes, in lukewarm water, in order to be fully enjoyed.

Back in the early 1980s, Kitti Cha Sangmanee and Richard Bueno hadn't yet realized it, either. During trips to discover tea-drinking habits across Europe, they noticed that everywhere people drank the same teas, made in the same way. It was during their apprenticeship in the trade, under the aegis of Marthe Cottin, that they learned the first basic rules: steeping time is not the same for whole-leaf black teas as it is for broken-leaf black teas, much less for green teas or blue teas. They also traveled to tea-growing countries such as China, Japan, and India, where they discovered not only the rich variety of leaves and methods of processing, but also the countless ways of preparing and appreciating tea. They returned with two guiding principles, ones that wonderfully suited their concept of "French tea."

First, there are no absolute, universal, definitive rules. The so-called purists—people who toss a contemptuous glance at anyone who adds a little sugar or a drop of milk to a cup of tea, indeed uses a little metal spoon or removes the leaves from the teapot after steeping—turn out to be ignorant, in fact. Everything is potentially possible and respectable when it comes to discovering tea's infinite savors. Tea leaves can be turned into a kind of chewing gum (as the Burmese do with *mieng*), yak butter can be added

> "Tea must be deserved;
> it is demanding. Every harvest
> has its own nature, its secrets.
> Tea is a noble beverage.
> Preparing it is an art that combines
> skill and tradition."
>
> **HENRI MARIAGE**

RIGHT *Flavored teas should preferably be steeped in a glass teapot—such as this Tango model in blown-glass—which, once washed, retains no trace of the specific flavor.*

to the brew (as Tibetans and Mongols do), and the same leaves can be steeped several times over (as the Chinese will tell you). These practices may not be appropriate everywhere in the world, but they are no more objectionable than adding sugar and milk in the British fashion.

Second—a principle that derives from the first—this diversity not only encourages tolerance and freedom but has also spurred Sangmanee and Bueno to develop their own preparation methods, which they have now passed on to their clients. Their original "tea-making guide" was a world first. It enabled customers to learn how to prepare various teas so that these highly select leaves could deliver all their potential. Obviously, Mariage Frères was not about to recommend adding yak butter to a Grand Yunnan, or to suggest pouring more hot water over used Chun Mee leaves, because its guide was not a treatise on the history and art of making tea everywhere in the world. Instead, it simply offered schooling, for anyone interested, in how to make the best possible tea. For example, Mariage Frères recommends removing the leaves from the pot as soon as the steeping time is over—a time that will vary depending on the type of tea—in order to prevent the tannins in the leaves from making the tea too bitter. And specialists suggest that *certain* teas can be taken with sugar or a drop of milk, for such additives not only won't denature these teas, they actually enhance certain specific qualities.

Mariage Frères' recommendations—fairly specific yet nuanced, in the spirit of French gastronomy—are enriched from year to year, in step with the experience of house specialists. Early customers perhaps recall that the first editions of the *Guide to Tea*, the precursor to *The French Art of Tea,* provided only brief advice—the 1984 recommendations occupied just half a page and made no distinction between the types of tea. Two years later, a full page was devoted to "the art of making tea." Customers were advised to use three different teapots, one for black teas, another for green teas, a third for flavored teas; furthermore, steeping times now varied according to the four basic families of tea. In 1988, the topic became a four-page chapter, and included a steeping table for various kinds of green Japan tea. These days, "The Art of Making Fine Tea" now runs to twelve pages, and the chapter describes various schools of tea preparation—in China, Japan, and Russia—as well as defining, through a few simple recommendations, the

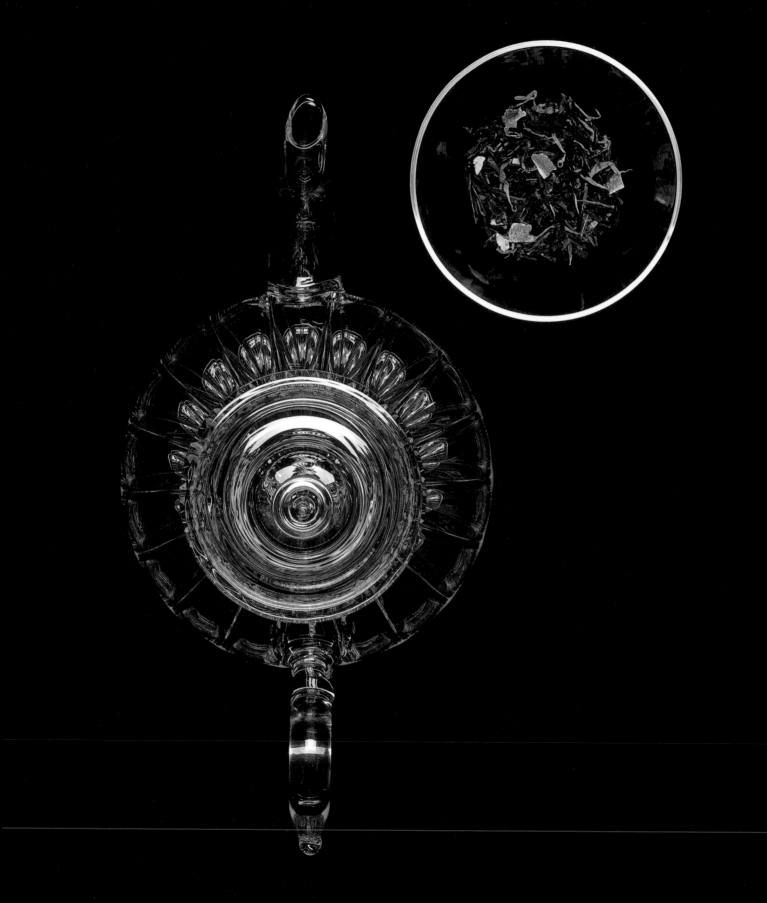

French art of making tea as invented by Mariage Frères. The French approach to tea is what French gastronomy is to cuisine: a set of guidelines adapted to each product in order to bring out its finest qualities, but which tea-lovers are entitled to break—at their own risk—in a spirit of creativity or personal taste. As with French gastronomy, heir to a wealth of foods and ingredients from all over the world, the French art of tea takes into account the considerable number and varieties of teas available at Mariage Frères outlets. In Japan, where the preparation and consumption of green tea gave rise to a strictly codified ceremony, the French rules have been generally adopted when it comes to black tea. An increasing number of Japanese now appreciate black tea and treat the Mariage Frères guidelines as though they represent a new, codified ceremony, called French tea—which they steep and serve, whenever possible, in teapots and cups designed by Mariage Frères.

The French art of making tea begins with water, for much depends upon that water. Should it contain a little chlorine or be too hard, it will alter the taste of the tea, which is highly sensitive to different qualities of water. That is why Sangmanee, when assessing the qualities of harvests and blends, systematically tastes them in three different ways in order to measure their potential and to learn how they will react. First he tastes the tea made with spring water, then with tap water, and finally with filtered water. Sometimes, in his Paris office-cum-lab, he discovers that a given harvest develops equally well with all three waters. But that is rarely the case. Since the quality of tap water can vary considerably, he usually recommends using soft mineral water or spring water.

The right water, heated to the right temperature (depending on the given tea) must then be poured into the right teapot (which has been heated in advance). That is because people who do not always drink the same tea should have several teapots on hand. Strong black teas—from Ceylon, Assam, Africa—develop best in a pot of porous material such as earthenware, pewter, or silver, which steadily becomes "seasoned." The finesse of Darjeelings, green, and blue teas, on the other hand, is best preserved in a pot with a smooth inner surface of porcelain, fine stoneware, enameled cast-iron, or glass. Flavored teas should be made in a glass teapot, which will retain no trace of a previous steeping and will therefore respect all the freshness of a new aroma. Finally, one teapot should be specially reserved for smoky teas. Only teapots of non-porous materials such as glass, porcelain, or fine stoneware can be washed—the others should simply be rinsed with running water, then turned upside down and set aside to dry.

Mariage Frères was determined to return the teapot to its noble status as a crucial accessory in making fine tea, which it did by inventing the enamel-lined cast-iron teapot in Japan, by adapting the legendary Yixing earthenware pot to modern use, and by designing nearly two hundred new models—as will be described in the next chapter. But perhaps the company's chief contribution to the art of tea has been its recommendation that leaves be withdrawn from the pot once the tea has steeped. People had acquired the habit of leaving them in the pot until it was empty—and sometimes even adding more water to those leaves to make more tea! This habit is not necessarily wrong in every case, particularly when it comes to lesser-quality teas, as currently practiced in China. But Mariage Frères wanted people to know that steeping leaves in the pot too long not only won't make the tea stronger, it actually damages the finer aspects of tea's flavor: over time, the tannin counteracts the stimulant chemical, theine, and adds a distinctly bitter taste. What might be acceptable for a dusty black tea trapped in a paper teabag becomes tragic when inflicted on a subtle leaf full of flavor and sensations. In order to make it easy to remove the leaves at the right moment, Mariage Frères recommends using a teapot with a built-in strainer, or to use a cotton filter (as opposed to a metal tea-ball, which does now allow the leaves to develop properly). In the same vein, Sangmanee's long experience in tasting teas the world over has enabled him to arrive at the perfect dose and ideal water temperature for each kind of tea.

Mariage Frères has henceforth published its "Five Golden Rules for Making Tea Successfully" along with an extremely detailed Steeping Chart that gives the amount of tea per cup, water temperature, and steeping time for each category of tea. Following these simple rules—along with the additional one of never drinking a fine tea boiling hot—will turn each cup of tea into a moment of pure bliss.

MARIAGE FRERES' FIVE GOLDEN RULES FOR MAKING TEA SUCCESSFULLY

BLACK TEAS, MATURED TEAS, BLUE—OR SEMI-OXIDIZED—TEAS, AND FLAVORED TEAS

1. Pre-heat the teapot, after inserting the tea strainer,* by rinsing it with boiling water.
2. Place a teaspoon of tea (roughly 2.5 g) per cup in the warm strainer* and let it stand for a few moments, allowing the steam to begin developing the leaves' aroma.
3. Pour simmering water on the tea so that all the leaves are covered.
4. Let the tea steep (see chart p. 141):
   - about 2 minutes for fannings
   - about 3 minutes for broken leaf teas
   - about 5 minutes for whole leaf teas
   - barely 3 minutes for first flush Darjeelings (slightly increasing the amount of tea to 3.5 g per cup)
   - 7 minutes for blue teas
5. It is then essential to remove the strainer or filter* containing the leaves. The tea must then be stirred (another important step) and finally poured. Teas from great estates should not be drunk too hot; let them stand a few moments after steeping, so that the palate can appreciate their subtle fragrances.

WHITE AND GREEN TEAS

1. Pre-heat the pot or *chung* (bowl with cover) as above.
2. Place the appropriate amount of tea per person or cup (refer to chart). Let the leaves stand for a few moments to allow the steam to begin developing the aroma.
3. Pour hot water onto the tea (refer to chart for exact temperature).
4. Let the tea steep (refer to chart):
   - 1 to 3 minutes for green tea
   - 15 minutes for white Yin Zhen
   - 7 minutes for white Pai Mu Tan
5. Remove the tea leaves, stir, and serve.

*Use a cotton tea taster filter if no strainer comes with the teapot.

BELOW AND RIGHT *The next steps entail adding pure water at just the right temperature, then removing the filter once the recommended steeping time has elapsed. Stir the tea before pouring it into the cup. Grand, costly teas should never be drunk too hot.*

MARIAGE FRÈRES' STEEPING CHART

TEA	AMOUNT*	WATER TEMPERATURE	AMOUNT OF WATER**	STEEPING TIME
White Tea Yin Zhen	5 g	158°F/70°C	20 cl	15 min.
White Teas Pai mu Tan	5 g	185°F/85°C	20 cl	7 min.
Finest Green Teas	5 g	158°F/70°C	20 cl	3 min.
Green Teas	5 g	203°F/95°C	20 cl	3 min.
Gyokuro n° T414	10 g	122°F/50°C	6 cl	2.5 min.
This tea should be prepared in tiny quantities and drunk from miniscule cups. It can be steeped three times.				
Green Japan Teas T416, T417, T418, T419, T4273, T4274, T4275, T4276, T4277, T4283	6.5 g	158°F/70°C	20 cl	2 min.
Green Japan Teas T421, T424, T426	4.5 g	194°F/90°C	20 cl	1 to 2 min.
Green Japan Teas T420, T422, T425	4.5 g	203°F/95°C	20 cl	1 min.
Blue Teas	2.5 g	203°F/95°C	20 cl	7 min.
Darjeeling First Flush	3.5 g	203°F/95°C	20 cl	3 min.
Whole Leaf Matured Teas and Black Teas	2.5 g	203°F/95°C	20 cl	5 min.
Broken Leaf Black Teas BOP and BPS and Black Pekoe Teas	2.5 g	203°F/95°C	20 cl	3 min.
Black Teas in Fanning BOPF	2.5 g	203°F/95°C	20 cl	2 min.
Flavored Teas	2.5 g	203°F/95°C	20 cl	3 to 5 min.

*1 g is approximately 0.0353 oz.

**20 cl of water is approximately 7 fluid ounces, or about one cup.

TEA WARE

The items on display in the impressive Tea Museum above the Mariage Frères tea house on Rue du Bourg-Tibourg, whether precious objects designed for aristocrats or wares for everyday use, testify to the talent of craftsmen of every period and every continent. Even in China, where tea has been the most common beverage for millennia, it has never been taken for granted—tea possesses so many virtues that it has earned the respect of people and the right to be handled with rare and costly utensils. Take, for example, the museum's porcelain tea services, made in China during the Tang dynasty: the blue of the porcelain, once filled with tea, transforms the amber color of the liquor into a precious jade green. Meanwhile, at Yixing in Jiangsu province, for the past five hundred years artisans have been making earthenware teapots, often shaped into marvelous forms, that are not only exquisitely smooth and extremely delicate in color, but are also among the best pots in which to steep tea. In Japan, cast-iron teapots were sometimes inlaid with gold decoration, while in Russia samovars might be of crystal or silver; in England, Sheffield tea services were examples of precious metalworking, while in France the remarkable artistry of royal porcelain manufactories yielded magnificent tea services. The list could go on and on, through examples of Art Nouveau and Art Deco accessories right down to contemporary designers, if there were space to include all the wonderful objects that tea-drinking has inspired throughout the world. And in addition to rare items, it is worth mentioning the efforts of generations of artisans who decorated the wooden chests that carried tea across the seas, the large metal canisters used by tea merchants, and the smaller tea caddies that stored tea in people's homes.

In 1982, when Richard Bueno and Kitti Cha Sangmanee first discovered Mariage Frères, they were immediately struck by the small collection of unusual items that the family had collected over two or three generations. These objects, the first pieces of the future museum, included a few Chinese shipping crates of various sizes, decorated with ideograms and sometimes made of precious woods, and an amazing collection of numbered containers originally used in a famous Paris shop called A La Porte Chinoise. Above all, however, the two men were delighted by the objects still used in the warehouse, objects that seemed to have been there for all time—brass scoops used to handle the tea leaves, old-fashioned scales, sifters, and so on. They reflected the profound nobility of a trade, indeed a whole world, that contrasted sharply

Grown on every continent, drunk in every country, tea has always favored encounters between great civilizations. Mariage Frères likes to encourage this dialogue by designing cross-cultural objects and experiences. A fine tea can be made in a Russian samovar and drunk from a Japanese tea service such as this gilded porcelain set made in Japan in the 19th century, probably for export.

with the mannered elegance of Parisian tearooms. So when the pair began to develop their idea of "French tea," they soon realized that accessories, whether costly or not, would have an important role to play. Objects should be designed in a spirit that paid tribute to a rare, delicious drink as well as evoking the simple nobility of a trade. The world they had already come to love, with its dreams, adventures, discoveries, and expertise, would be all the more accessible to people if Mariage Frères also sold the right accessories. Such items should be made available to everyone rather than confined to fancy tearooms, they should be designed to withstand offshore winds rather than flaunt pretty floral patterns. The idea of designing objects was not only a logical progression for the firm, it also reflected the men's aesthetic temperaments, notably Sangmanee's artistic talents, which were still seeking an outlet.

In the spring of 1983, when the two men were considering the idea of serving certain teas, on special occasions, in the warehouse on Rue du Cloître-Saint-Merri, the young Sangmanee was brought up short on seeing a 1920s-style teapot in an antique shop. At the time he was fascinated by Art Deco and the Bauhaus style, and he frequented not only antique dealers but museums and libraries, including the library in the Musée des Arts Décoratifs, where he would go several times a week. He liked the pure, universal lines of modern art, the timeless look that, some fifty years earlier, had eliminated finicky detail from the design of objects, furniture, and jewelry. Furthermore, this 1920s-and-30s look—because it extended much further than the graceful prettiness usually associated with conventional tea salons, because it was simultaneously straightforward and highly elegant, and because it still evoked a colonial era with its hint of adventure—perfectly suited the idea of the French art of tea. Sangmanee's eye was therefore drawn to that teapot like a magnet. It was of pure, white porcelain, simple and round in shape, and furthermore had a useful feature that might have startled a stuffy old English lady—a metal globe that covered it, to keep the heat in. Bueno was also delighted by this teapot. The two men contemplated not only using it on Rue

BELOW AND RIGHT *Cactus and "1920": two limited-edition*
teapots designed by Mariage Frères, hand-decorated
with Art-Deco motifs at the enamelware factory in Longwy.

du Cloître-Saint-Merri but reproducing the model and selling it. First they did some documentary research. They discovered that it had been designed around 1925, inspired by the functionalist aesthetics of the Bauhaus and the Swiss architect Le Corbusier. The teapot had been distributed in several European countries, where it had not been sold directly but was awarded as a free gift by certain department stores if a given sum was spent there. In fact, it was not all that unusual for examples of it to turn up in the stalls of antique dealers. Just a few weeks later Sangmanee even glimpsed one in a scene of a movie by Jean-Jacques Beineix, *Moon in the Gutter,* which had just been released.

Reproducing the teapot, on the other hand, proved to be much trickier. The original manufacturer had disappeared, and craftsmen able to work both metal and porcelain were few and far between. Finally, the original maker was tracked down, and a reproduction of the "Art Deco 1930" teapot saw the light of day on Rue du Cloître-Saint-Merri in early 1985. It came in two sizes, and was immediately popular. Later it was produced in two additional colors, black for smoky teas and blue for flavored teas. This teapot is still emblematic of Mariage Frères today, used in their tearooms and sold regularly in their stores.

Given this initial success, the company launched an entire series of reproductions—always slightly revised—of teapots and tea services from that classic period of design. Some of them required multiple voyages undertaken by Sangmanee, often accompanied by Bueno and later Desains, in search of manufacturers able to make his dreams come true. Miraculous discoveries were sometimes countered by disappointments, such as the Luxembourg factory that had failed to save the molds for a very fine green and gold tea service produced in the 1920s. But Mariage Frères had the molds remade, dubbed the service Glamour, and had another hit on its hands. A "mestizo" service called Métis, meanwhile, also in an Art

Deco vein, was the product of a collaboration between Sangmanee and a Mariage Frères customer who, as chance would have it, had bought an enamel works in Longwy, France. Thanks to the new owner's archives and to her enthusiasm, the black-and-yellow Métis service was produced, as were limited editions of several other teapots from the same period.

In 1986 there began yet another venture that would lead Mariage Frères from a simple idea to a revolution in the world of tea (and even to making a mark beyond that world). The story took place in Japan, where Bueno had gone to explore several tea plantations. He also decided to visit the Morioka region to the north, which specialized in the production of cast-iron utensils. Since he had already organized several Japanese tea ceremonies in Paris alongside Sangmanee, he was familiar with the fine cast-iron kettles used to boil water in Japan. Called *chanoy-gamai,* they first appeared in the fourteenth century, during the Muromachi era, and attained a high level of refinement, whether decorated with figurative motifs in relief or with a wonderfully coarse grain. Some of them were even inlaid with gold, silver, or copper, and presented to Japanese lords by vassals seeking protection; in Japan, sturdy and indestructible cast-iron is perceived as a symbol of power and authority. This impression of strength struck the people at Mariage Frères, for it is unusual in the normally delicate world of tea. It occurred to them that, like Art Deco items, cast-iron accessories could overcome the effete image of that world, and might appeal to younger, more masculine customers. Hence the idea of making teapots—rather than kettles, which would have a hard time finding a niche in French kitchens—of cast-iron. So Bueno wanted to find out whether Japanese craftsmen actually made teapots in that metal.

Once he found himself in the heart of Japan's cast-iron producing region, he was amazed by the age-old skills still used on a very small scale, by families that worked in their old wooden homes, selling their

> *"Many men and young people are uncomfortable with tea's traditional association with 'flowery china.' So what we liked about cast-iron, in addition to its sturdiness, was its masculine nobility and handsomeness. We're determined to continue to recruit new tea-drinkers."*
>
> **KITTI CHA SANGMANEE**

output to cooperatives. There were plenty of kettles and various decorative objects, but no teapots in sight. After several encounters, Bueno finally found a craftsman willing to listen to his crazy idea: Bueno wanted a teapot of cast-iron in a Western size (the Japanese themselves make tea in tiny recipients) and he wanted the inside lined with enamel to avoid altering the taste of the tea. In short, he wanted this craftsman, heir to a timeless tradition, to produce a totally original item. Several months and several trials later, Mariage Frères publicly presented the first cast-iron teapots at its Festival of Japanese Tea. Shortly afterward, during another trip to Japan in the company of Franck Desains, the question of color was raised. The first teapots had been the same color as Japanese kettles, a someone dreary and monotonous black or brown. But in Japan, the two men noticed that workshops produced various other cast-iron items—bells, amulets, weights for scrolls of calligraphy—in a range of handsome reds and golds with a fine patina of age. They were told, however, that in Japan the kettles used in the tea ceremony never came in those colors, so why should the teapots be so bold? Bueno and Desains insisted. It was not a question here of tradition, for which they had enormous respect, but of broadening Japanese culture by creating a hybrid teapot. As soon as Japanese craftsmen understood, they made cast-iron teapots in reds, blues, and greens, often with a fine patina. Since the initial teapots were all more or less the same shape, the next step involved designing new models. That is how Mariage Frères' classic line of cast-iron teapots came into being, christened with evocative names such as Pleine Lune (Full Moon), Gouverneur, etc., and collectively known as La Voie du Thé (The Way of Tea).

Back at Mariage Frères, these teapots were extraordinarily popular. Soon other tea merchants wanted to sell them. Various new companies were specially set up to import them. Dozens of other Japanese craftsmen began supplying this new demand, initially French but soon international. That is how the cast-iron teapot, redesigned by Mariage Frères, met with worldwide success and revitalized an entire region of Japan. At Mariage Frères they often say, with a wry smile, that they should have patented the design. . . . However, the firm is mainly proud not of triggering an international fashion, nor of rejuvenating still further

the image of tea-drinking, nor even of having contributed to the economic development of an entire region, but rather of having devised an accessory that is now irrevocably linked to the concept of French-style tea. These teapots are even popular in Japan, where they are known as "French teapots" yet are viewed as a worthy interpretation of Japanese culture, as is Sakura tea.

This story even has a second chapter. During yet another trip to Japan in 1987, Bueno discovered wonderful little cups made of glass-paste, used for drinking cold sake. They had no handles, and were very delicate yet felt very natural. They were produced by a family of outstanding glassmakers. Since their lightness and finesse could provide a kind of balance to a tea service built around a cast-iron teapot, Bueno thought they might be perfect for drinking tea. But only if they could withstand the heat, and would not be stained by the tannin in tea. After having tested them, Bueno mulled over the idea, met the glass-makers, and suggested that a small leaf of unburnished gold be included in the glass-paste, providing a touch of mystery. The resulting glasses, born of two cultures, met with great success in both France and Japan. In that latter country, it has become unthinkable to employ a "French teapot" without its accompanying glass teacups—the whole service has become an overall concept. And once again the craftsmen have profited by exporting their wares throughout the entire world.

The amazing popularity of teapots in cast-iron freed Mariage Frères from its constant concern to present tea-drinking in a different light, to win over recalcitrant customers such as males and young people. By 1987, this mission had been accomplished. At which point the firm's three designers could give free

rein to their imagination and whimsy. In the late 1980s, Mariage Frères was offering twelve new models of teapot for sale every year, a pace all the more impressive in that every single one was designed in-house. In this sphere, the creativity of the Mariage team operated in the same way as it did for the composition of teas or the design of boxes and packaging—that is to say, in total liberty, with no fear of violating certain traditions that had become routine. It is probable that this freedom of thought and action was partly due to the backgrounds of the three men, which made them open to the world's diversity (Desains, as will be described in a subsequent chapter, grew up in Africa and had a Franco-Chinese mother). Such freedom jostled old habits. At the time, for instance, the almost miraculous multiplication of Mariage Frères teapots and the company's recommendation that tea-drinkers use several teapots, one for each kind of tea, considerably upset porcelain manufacturers who were accustomed to designing complete services with a single teapot (that naturally matched the cups), viewed as a unique, ever-present part of the family tea ceremony. The liberty and flexibility in choice of teapots, as required by demands of the quality and variety of Mariage Frères teas, revolutionized the traditional concept of tea service.

Numerous illustrations could be given of the freedom with which the Mariage Frères designers have since produced teapots, among other items. Desains, for example, highly enamored of the English lifestyle and familiar with England and Scotland—notably with the antique dealers and second-hand shops there—decided to rethink the traditional, silver-plated Sheffield teapots so hallowed in Britain since the eighteenth century. As usual, his thinking did not yield a straightforward reproduction, but rather a

Sheffield-style teapot made of Limoges china! Or, to be more precise, Limoges biscuit-ware, that is to say unglazed porcelain, the color being added to the porcelain paste itself. The change in material so transformed the teapot, which inaugurated a line called Métissage Anglais (English Blend), that it constituted a truly new creation. The line now includes one of the firm's most amusing items, namely the "Monsieur Mariage" mustache cup, with a rectangular opening for sipping the tea—it represents a nod to Henri Mariage, the company's mustachioed founder, who used such a cup (which was fairly common at the time) to taste his teas without wetting his whiskers.

Of over two hundred teapots designed to date, the ones that are true reproductions can be counted on the fingers of one hand. The magnificent Karawan is among these, however. This legendary teapot, made either of solid silver or silver-plate, has become a Mariage Frères classic—the main body takes the-form of a seated camel, being loaded by a camel-driver who serves as handle. It was Sangmanee who discovered the original model for this teapot in the Victoria and Albert Museum in London. It dates from 1875, the high period of orientalism, and was rather coarse in manufacture, being a golden-hued red earthenware. Sangmanee, that inspired teapot-designer, immediately thought about reproducing it in silver. But it wasn't signed, which meant that no archival trace of it could be found. He therefore used photos from the museum catalogue to produce an initial prototype in silver—which was subsequently stolen from the Mariage Frères museum! But a limited edition of the teapot was produced, to satisfy the numerous customers who fell in love with this unusual item, which—in honor of oriental caravans—Sangmanee dubbed the Karawan.

A second great saga, following on from Japan, dawned in the early 1990s. For several years, Mariage Frères had been wondering about selling legendary teapots as fascinating as they were inaccessible— namely, earthenware teapots made at Yixing, in the Chinese province of Jiangsu. They have been produced there since the sixteenth century, and were once extensively imported into Europe along with cargoes of tea in the seventeenth and eighteenth centuries. Then they dropped out of sight. They are made of a more or less shiny brownish earthenware, also known as boccaro, which "seasons" well with repeated use, and is marvelous for steeping black teas. The high cost of these teapots—even in China—stems from the technique employed to obtain their color, derived not from the addition of pigments but from the careful

> *"We spent days rummaging through the archives and workshops of the Yixing factory. On coming across ancient teapots, ideas for new models sprang to mind. In the end, I gave them sketches for sixteen teapots, which they agreed to manufacture."*
>
> **FRANCK DESAINS**

mixture of clays from different seams to produce the desired shade: brownish, greenish, reddish. The clay being relatively easy to work, over the centuries these teapots have been given a multitude of forms, many being very tiny in size, as suited to the Chinese tea ceremony. Sangmanee knew that no better clay could be found for earthenware teapots, and that manufactories still existed at Yixing, but in those days China remained a closed country. The teapots he had been shown in official export bureaus, allegedly from Yixing, were sold so cheaply that he knew they couldn't be made from the authentic clay. He therefore waited until he was able to get to Yixing himself, once Deng Xiaoping's policy of opening China to the world economy had begun to bear fruit, allowing foreigners to travel more freely within the country.

Sangmanee's first trip to Yixing took place in 1991. He and Desains went to a large state factory, which thereby received its first foreign buyers. Management treated them royally, inviting them to an extraordinary banquet. They remained on the site for three days, observing the age-old methods of manufacture, examining stocks, nosing around old collections and archives in search of models that might suit them. As it transpired, the teapots then being made there were too small and overly decorated with animals and flowers, and were therefore light years away from their idea of the French art of tea. On coming across several models in the archives, however, Desains was able to design on the spot—using a notebook he always keeps to hand when travelling—sixteen teapots suited to preparing tea the French way. The factory director agreed to produce them, and they became the first elements of the line christened A la Porte Chinoise, the "Chinese Gate" being the name of a famous oriental-goods shop in Paris in the nineteenth century. These teapots came in various shapes and colors, some being traditional, others revamped. One, however, was a perfect reproduction, namely the extraordinary Gémeaux (Twin), comprising a twin-compartment pot separated by a filter to keep the leaves from the already steeped tea. The largest of the new teapots, the Marco Polo, was based on an early eighteenth-century model (during the Manchurian Qing dynasty), brought up to date by the addition of a filter and a brass handle. This line was difficult to sell at first, because the French think of earthenware as an ordinary, inexpensive material. The people at Mariage

BELOW *L'Heure du Thé gift box. Mariage Frères' boxes, canisters,*
and packaging create a pure graphic image that is immediately recognizable.
RIGHT *The large, 2.5-kilogram canisters with numbers are hand-painted*
reproductions—customized for Mariage Frères—of ones used at the famous
oriental-goods store, À la Porte Chinoise (now in the Tea Museum).

MARIAGE FRÈRES
Maison de Thé à Paris
depuis 1854

SAKURA

Thé vert parfumé
aux fleurs de cerisier

SUPERIOR CHOICEST
SELECTED
NEW SEASON'S

No. MF 1

SPRING 2000

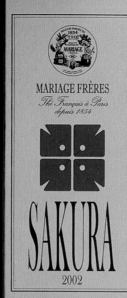

MARIAGE FRÈRES
Maison de Thé à Paris
depuis 1854

SAKURA

Thé vert parfumé
aux fleurs de cerisier

SUPERIOR CHOICEST
SELECTED
NEW SEASON'S

No. MF 1

SPRING 2001

MARIAGE FRÈRES
Thé Français à Paris
depuis 1854

SAKURA

2002

Thé vert parfumé aux fleurs de cerisier
Green tea flavoured with cherry blossoms

MARIAGE FRÈRES
Thé Français à Paris
depuis 1854

SAKURA

2003

Thé vert parfumé aux fleurs de cerisier
Green tea flavoured with cherry blossoms

BEL AMI

MARIAGE FRÈRES

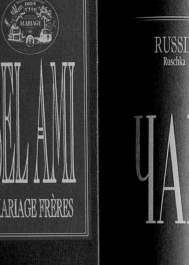

RUSSI
Ruschka

ЧА

MARIAGE F

NIL

ROUGE

THÉ ROUGE
MARIAGE FRÈRES

THÉ FRANÇAIS
A PARIS DEPUIS 1854

FALL
IN
LOVE

THÉ
MARIAGE FRÈRES

MARCO
POLO

THÉ NOIR

MARIAGE FRÈRES

THÉ FRANÇAIS
À PARIS DEPUIS 1854

MARIAGE FRÈRES
Thé Français à Paris
depuis 1854

ROUGE
D'AUTOMNE

Thé rouge parfumé aux fruits d'automne
Red tea flavoured with autumn fruits

MARIAGE FRÈRES

EARL GREY

FRENCH

BLUE

MARIAGE FR
Thé Français à
depuis 1854

TH
DE
PÂQU

THÉ NOIR FEST
FESTIVE TEA FOR EASTER C

Frères, though, knew that customers would eventually realize why these special teapots, handmade from rare clay, were so costly. Still unique, they are absolutely ideal for serving excellent black teas.

Returning to the Art Deco 1930 teapot, the first—and most famous—ever produced by Mariage Frères, it became the cornerstone of the Retro-Colonial line. Every year new models were added to this line, usually of porcelain and always exotic, adventurous, and imaginative, summing up the Mariage Frères spirit. As ever, they were given evocative titles, in the manner of a poem or painting. This line yielded some great classics, such as the Navigateur service, with its pure round shapes hosting a decoration that harks back to the exotic "tea route" that ran from Shanghai to Le Havre. Another popular model is the Rangoon, a teapot inspired by a voyage to the Golden Triangle, with an elegantly fluted body draped in the bold plum color of the sarongs worn by Burmese women during festive celebrations; as already noted so often, Sangmanee frequently draws inspiration from his travels. It was during another voyage, this time to Japan, that the sight of an eighteenth-century incense holder gave him an idea for a magical, multi-lobed teapot of ivory porcelain, endowed with a cast-iron top that was specially pierced to allow the tea's aroma to rise in scented plumes. He naturally dubbed it the Brûle-Parfum, or "Scent Holder." This simple, wonderful idea embodies the company's concern, right from the start, for the multiple sensory pleasures of tea. At the same time, it illustrates this line's strong tendency to combine materials—and cultures—in a bold, new way. To take another example, the teapot called Aventurier, whose oval shape was inspired by the small hand-warmers used in China, weds a bamboo handle to a porcelain pot. This handle had to be specially made, at Desains' request, by a craftsman in a small village in Japan. In the same way, the magnificent Opium teapot successfully marries a simple, sturdy lid of pewter to fine, delicate porcelain.

Tea needs to be beheld by the eye and smelled with the nose, as well as tasted on the palate, or even imagined in the fragrant darkness of its hermetic container. The importance of such containers in the history of tea becomes clear on entering the Mariage Frères museum. Artists and craftsmen have always been inspired to produce large handsome canisters for tea merchants, and fine small tins for home use. By devising new containers, Bueno, Sangmanee, and Desains were respecting a tradition established by the Mariage brothers themselves—most of the ones on display in the museum came from the warehouse on Rue du Cloître-Saint-Merri (such as the large numbered canisters—from one to forty-eight—purchased

BELOW *Tea caddies in the Coupole line illustrate the ongoing evolution of the firm's visual image.*

by the company from the famous oriental-goods shop, A La Porte Chinoise). The new design team, however, wanted to enrich this tradition with a concern to give tea a packaging worthy of its quality and status. Having already invested heavily in discovering and composing the finest teas possible, Mariage Frères was determined to devote the same energy to the design of objects in which it would be stored. A wonderful tea should be wonderfully packaged.

The now-famous 2.5 kilogram black-and-yellow canisters juggled by the clerks behind the counters of Mariage Frères tea houses were designed in 1984, along with a 100-gram version (perfect for aromatic gifts of Route du Temps, Marco Polo, Pleine Lune, and some thirty other teas), and the little black paper bags. The work of Bueno and Sangmanee, these designs radically altered the standard packaging for tea, up until then restricted to colors traditionally associated with luxury goods or with China, namely red and gold. The drastic choice of black—which would become highly fashionable several years later—was deliberately provocative in an effort to appeal, once again, to people not usually part of that world. The black packaging was so successful and became so identified with the Mariage Frères image that the company felt no need to devise other containers for many years. It nevertheless reproduced certain large canisters on display in the museum, including the numbered series from A La Porte Chinoise, comprising a line of items called Marchand de Thé (Tea Merchant). All these containers were made to order, painted by hand, and each required thirty hours of labor. In 1993, fresh from exploring China, the house designers could not resist the temptation to re-create earthenware tea jars of yore, retaining the same shape but miniaturizing the size and giving them a satiny lacquer finish. One of them contained that year's Noël tea, and they are still used to market festive teas.

No further innovations followed until the year 2000. In that highly symbolic year of change and transition, Sangmanee and Desains decided to bring a breath of fresh air to their series of containers. With their usual sense of freedom, they designed several new lines of containers of varied inspiration, adding splashes of color to Mariage Frères tea houses and putting a smile on the new millennium. Once again, the firm's non-conformism ruffled some feathers. All professionals in the packaging industry, for example, are told that blue containers are strongly discouraged when it comes to food items. This mysterious dictate has no real basis, but had become a golden rule in the industry—which Mariage Frères blithely broke. In

BELOW *Tinted glass jars in the Tea Club line each contain a select tea from Thailand.*

the months that followed, the Tea Club line boldly proclaimed the firm's penchant for a blending of cultures—a totally English name for a French-style selection of six outstanding teas from Thailand. Each tea was sold in a glass jar tinted with its special color: yellow for Chai Thai, orchid blue for Thai Beauty, black for Opium Hill, velvety red for Siam Club, pale green for Lan Na Thai, and royal blue for Bouddha Bleu. This poetic line was dedicated to the fertile riches of Sangmanee's home country. The same tones would later decorate tall, cylindrical containers in metal, covered with paper and endowed with a double lid, dressing flavored blends in fresh hues of orange, fuchsia, violet, and pale blue. Six of them were adorned with the word "tea" written in the language of its place of origin.

This idea soon gave birth to a line of lacquered metal containers embellished with the word "tea" decoratively written in twelve languages representing the twelve cultures where tea originated or was developed. It took three years of work to produce all twelve of them. Sangmanee and Desains did not simply want to copy the words as found in a book or dictionary, but sought an original, perfect calligraphy for each one. Desains therefore wound up calligraphing them himself. It was particularly difficult, for example, to devise a calligraphic version of Singhalese—for Ceylon teas—that was both attractive and accurate. The choice of colors—a different one for each container—also required a certain amount of time. Some seemed obvious from the start—such as the plum-colored sarongs for Burmese tea, and the silver of the prayer wheels for Tibetan tea—but what color was appropriate for Arabia? Desains, who found the Arabic

BELOW *Four of the twelve containers in the Calligraphies*
du Thé line, each representing a tea-producing or tea-drinking
culture. In addition to being decoratively innovative,
each metallic container presents a new blend
based on a tea typical of the given country or region.

PRECEDING PAGES *Measuring spoons and strainers of horn, wood, and metal.*
RIGHT *Made by hand, one by one, cotton muslin bags hold whole-leaf
tea without crushing it, unlike the industrial paper variety.
They allow the tea to develop fully, and in no way alter the flavor.*

writing for the word "tea" to be extremely modern, opted for the timeless modernity of white. Initially, the containers in this line of "tea calligraphy" were to be sold empty, but slowly the idea arose that the new tins, visually very different from traditional Mariage Frères containers, could also be used to promote new blends. To evoke each tea-growing country, Sangmanee composed blends of teas based on the local variety, while for tea-drinking cultures he opted for typical associations such as a mint-and-fruit flavored tea for Arabia, called Thé des Rois (Tea of Kings).

It is not possible to list the countless accessories designed or reproduced by Mariage Frères since its rebirth in 1982. They have all been devised in-house, usually at the initiative and under the supervision of Sangmanee, never with the help of outside design or style agencies. The only exception to this rule is the line of pewter accessories created by Japanese designer Toshiyuki Kita, comprising several glass tea containers and two teapots. As a fan of Mariage Frères, Kita designed them specially with the French tea merchant in mind, and then showed up one day to present his designs. Sangmanee and Desains found them so beautiful that they included the items in their catalogue. Alongside basic utensils—tea services and containers—the company has also designed numerous bowls, glasses, saucers, tea stands, strainers, and dosers, not to mention the magnificent packaging of certain products such as tea-flavored sweet biscuits, cotton-muslin teabags, tea jellies, and gift boxes (handsome objects in themselves), all designed by Desains. These accessories make Mariage Frères much more than just a tea merchant; it has become a dynamic workshop where ideas are mooted, take shape, assume a form, and are tested. Here, the freewheeling, international spirit of the French approach to tea has created objects that are worthy servants of the beverage that Mariage Frères hopes everyone will love and appreciate.

6 FRAGRANCES OF TEA

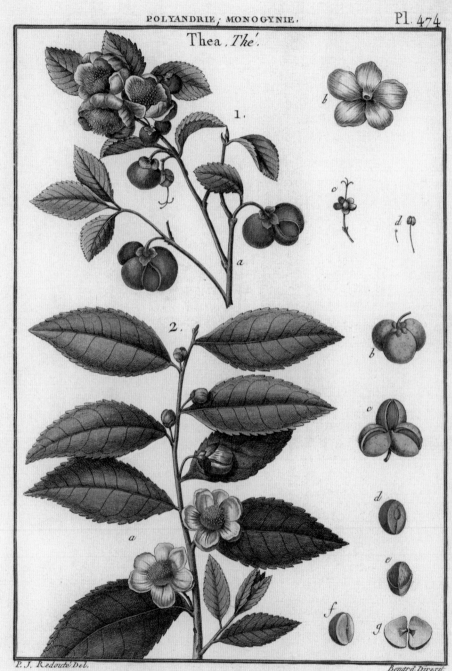

Thea, *Thé*.

HISTOIRE NATURELLE, *Botanique*.

P. J. Redouté Del.

Benard Direxit

237.

LEFT $\mathcal{A}$ 19th-century botanical drawing of "Camellia sinensis."
The tea plant contains natural, highly subtle flavor molecules.
PRECEDING PAGE $\mathcal{A}$ delicate aromatic harmony is created
by a steaming Brûle-Parfum teapot, a stick of incense,
a candle, and the leaves of a flowery tea.

In 1987, just after Mariage Frères had moved to its current premises on Rue du Bourg-Tibourg, a young tea fancier who had become a regular customer back on Rue du Cloître-Saint-Merri finally left the production company where he was employed in order to accept a full-time job working with Kitti Cha Sangmanee and Richard Bueno. At the time, Franck Desains was twenty-six years old. He had gone to business school, but his fertile imagination and his skilled draftsmanship made him a natural and active participant in the design projects brilliantly launched by Mariage Frères. Soon, however, most of his time would be devoted to one particular sector—creating tea-based scents. This idea sprang from his own personal background. Desains, whose father was French and whose mother was Franco-Chinese, was born in black Africa. He lived in Cameroon until the age of seventeen, and he accompanied his parents in their travels across the land in search of native peoples such as the Bamum, the Bamileke, and the Peul. He often scampered along the slopes of Mount Cameroon, a volcano where magnificent tea estates were planted. His African childhood endowed Desains with a taste for diversity in people and places, with a taste for tea, and also with a taste for savors and scents. In this latter realm, his taste was more than a penchant—he had always wanted to become a perfumer, and at the age of seven or eight he was already composing unusual aromatic blends based on various plants and spices.

So when Desains first entered the Mariage Frères premises in 1984, this fan of English-style black tea was instantly struck by the amazing fragrance of all those teas combined. Later, once he began working for the company, he learned the history of the Mariage family, notably that of Aimé, Marthe Cottin's great-grandfather, who had induced the firm to make and sell candles. Thus, thanks to the convergence of two personal histories, and after a few years of gestation, the idea of a tea-scented candle was born.

The idea may seem pretty standard today. But in 1987 it was completely original. No one had ever thought of creating a fragrance based on *Camellia sinensis* even though tea releases some of the most exquisite and subtle scent molecules in the world. So new was the idea that it entailed commercial risk, but it was nevertheless immediately backed by Bueno and Sangmanee. In developing the French art of tea, the two men were innovating and rejuvenating an entire scene in an ongoing way, and candles seemed to fit that pattern perfectly. The initial idea, developed collectively, was to re-create the wonderful scent of the five hundred teas impregnating the Rue du Bourg-Tibourg premises. There was something fun and witty about it. The team would attempt to allow customers to walk out of the store not only with their favorite tea, but also with a few delightful whiffs of the magical fragrance of the place. That magic would be re-created through the most seductive of symbols, a scented flame. Mariage Frères' most impalpable treasure, one that had never yet left home—its distinctive odor—would now go forth and travel the world. It was a gamble worth making.

With the help of a professional "nose"—one of Mariage Frères' young customers who has since become a great name in her profession—Desains got down to work. The two alchemists spent months opening canisters of tea, smelling them, steeping the leaves, wetting them, rubbing them, drying them, tirelessly hunting down the odiferous molecules in order to combine them or compare them to similar molecules in other plants. After a whole year of trials and some twenty failed attempts, the right candle finally saw the light of day. It was dubbed Thé des Pluies (Tea of Rains), because its scent, which accurately corresponded to the complex fragrances of the shop, also evoked the rich smells of a tea estate after the rain, with its damp leaves, moist earth, thick mosses, and blossoming flowers. The scent was not light but gentle, not too thick, simultaneously masculine and feminine, perfectly expressing the spirit of Mariage Frères. Desains therefore decided to color it chestnut brown, and placed it in a fine tinted glass holder of silky black, engraved with the Mariage Frères logo, which shimmered in the flickering light of the flame.

The world's first tea-scented candle, Thé des Pluies carried the fragrance of Mariage Frères to every continent. People who smelled it for the first time adored the fragrance that filled every nook of their home not only because it was so pleasant, but also because it resembled no other fragrance. Thé des Pluies represented a radical break with ordinary scented candles, which were designed to imitate the odor of a flower or spice. In contrast, the Mariage Frères candle evoked an entire universe, a whole landscape of tea-related smells, thereby triggering the same emotions stimulated by that landscape. This candle was designed not only to scent an interior, but to generate sensations that went beyond olfactory pleasure. Customers immediately sensed this difference and saw to it that Thé des Pluies was an enormous hit.

The story of tea-scented candles might have ended there, with this triumph. It had been conceived as a unique item. The magic of the fragrance of the Mariage Frères tea house could now travel everywhere, the goal had been attained. Desains didn't think about candles again for the next four or five years. They were

RIGHT *Thé Blanc candles evoke the fragrance of flowers
that scent the rarest and most private Chinese gardens where
white tea is harvested. A year of research and experimentation
was required to reconstitute that sublime fragrance faithfully.*

creative years, years of traveling to plantations and discovering the wonderful variety of smells associated with tea. And it was finally tea itself that spurred him to have another try. The subtle odors of tea were so varied that it suddenly seemed a shame to limit them to a single candle. China, where he often traveled, awakened forgotten but suddenly familiar sensations in Desains, and its tradition of green jasmine tea prompted him to devise another scented candle, Thé des Mandarins. This "Tea of Mandarins" candle was accompanied by a third one, Thé Rouge, or "Red Tea," which evoked the overtones of gingerbread, honey, and vanilla already associated with a combination of two of the firm's teas, the famous Marco Polo and a Bourbon red tea. Once again, getting the fragrances for these two new candles just right required months of research and testing.

Candle fans had to wait another few years before the range was extended further. Indeed, it took a long time to develop the next two scents. Both were the extremely complex outcome of different experiences, and both involved the ongoing collaboration between Sangmanee, Desains, and certain Darjeeling planters. For both represented a tribute to these wonderful Indian tea gardens at the foot of the Himalaya Mountains. The candle called Darjeeling developed the same subtle, ineffable grace of the aroma of Darjeeling teas, with their slightly sweet and bitter notes, their hints of woodiness and green almond, of hazelnut and muscatel. The candle was colored pale green and set in a satiny glass. The other candle, Rose d'Himalaya, stemmed from Sangmanee's work with the Arya estate in Darjeeling, in an effort to produce, on a regular basis, the striking aroma of rose that one of the plots on the estate seemed to produce spontaneously. In studying this strange phenomenon, Sangmanee and Desains discovered that the tea and rose plants both have a similar aromatic molecule, which increases in tea according to the amount of sunlight, the quality of the soil, and the way the leaves are processed. Desains wanted to re-create this special alchemy in the Rose d'Himalaya candle, so graceful and light that it seems like a rosebud floating in its cloudy gray glass.

Rose d'Himalaya is a good illustration of the way Mariage Frères candles are born of a tea-related experience, feeling, or discovery. They might be called *auteur* candles, in the way that highly personal, artistic French movies are called *auteur* films. That is probably what makes them so popular, as reconfirmed in 2001 when the company introduced four new candles. The one inspired by white tea, Thé Blanc, is a good example. The idea for this candle came to Desains while on a Chinese estate that plucks only leaves of exceptionally high quality, which are then merely withered and dried, undergoing no other processing, and sold as "white" tea (a category invented by Sangmanee). At the moment of plucking, these leaves give off a striking flowery smell that is particularly strong if you stick your nose into a bamboo basket full of them. Which is just what Desains did, recording in his little notebook all the feelings that this scent produced in him. When an idea for a scent comes to him this way, during a trip—which is a frequent occurrence— he describes his perceptions in great detail. Since he is not a professional "nose," and has not acquired all the technical vocabulary of that trade, he employs a range of subtle olfactory metaphors relating to more or less ripe fruits, flowers of different varieties, and sundry evocative odors. These are the impressions that he will convey to the professional nose with whom he works so that, together, the pair can arrive at

the final product, following a series of tests. All this patient labor went into the making of Thé Blanc, a candle that projects the floral magic of a legendary tea.

Because the major tea-producing countries are also lands of incense, and because tea and incense are closely linked in the imaginative minds of Desains and Sangmanee, both men tend to burn the most precious, aromatic incense at home. So it is hardly surprising that one day they embarked on a new adventure, this time involving incense. They didn't have the slightest idea how Mariage Frères customers would react to this latest incarnation of their obsession for tea. As usual, the two men made no attempt to conduct market surveys or consumer studies. They simply wanted to create an incense that didn't yet exist—which was reason enough for doing it. They were thinking of a very limited range of only three scents, each of which would

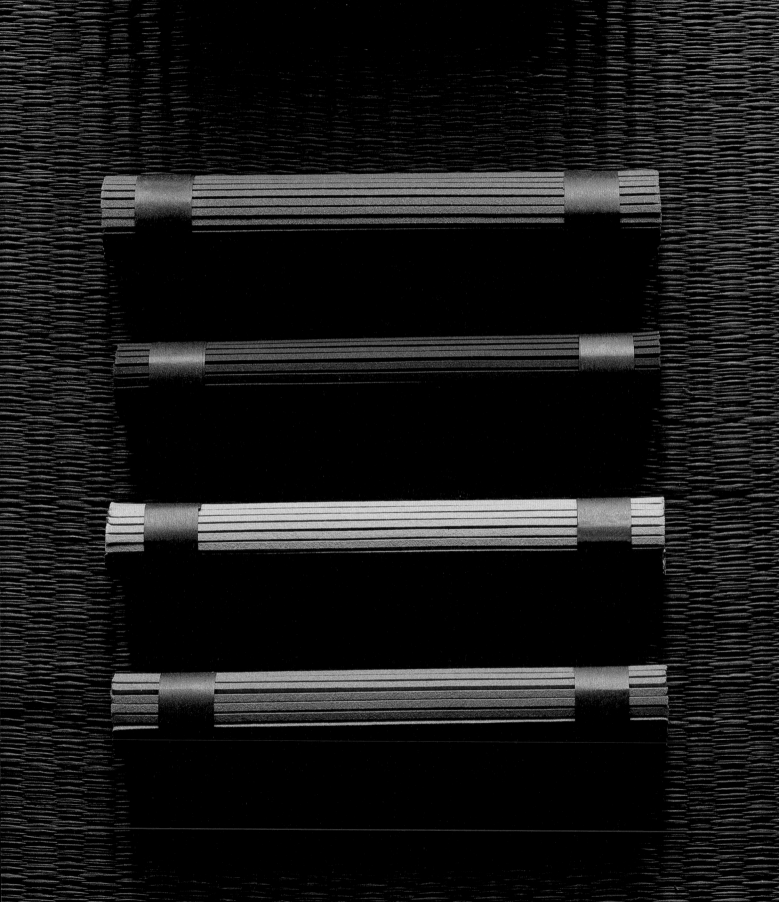

deliver a specifically fragrant moment in a high-altitude tea garden, because each day unfolds in a sequence of changing scents as well as changing light. These three scents would trace that evolution, from morning sweetness to daytime strength to evening mystery. There would be an incense for morning, when the first rays of sunlight burn the mist and awaken all the odors of damp earth and leaves still moist with dew; there would be another stick for midday, when the leaves plucked the previous day are processed in the workshops as the sun beats down on the wooden walls, so that the odor of drying leaves mingles with the smell of warm wood; and there would be an incense for nighttime when, beneath the pale light of a full moon, still other moist fragrances drench the garden—subtle, secret, mysterious scents that emerge from the blend of shadow and light, amplified by the echo of darkness.

But the men's concept of this ideal series of incense, one that would evoke a sequence of magic moments, was so demanding that they searched for several long years before they found anyone capable of producing it. They eventually eliminated India and China, where incense tends to be too strong, and began scouring Japan, a land where incense is so refined that it has become the object of a veritable discipline, a "way" or "path" like the ones associated with flower arranging and tea appreciation. Sangmanee and Desains liked the fact that, in Japan, people talked about "listening to" incense rather than "smelling" it—listening to what the incense is trying to say, understanding what it is trying to express. This approach was similar to the one that had inspired the production of Mariage Frères candles: not just to create a scent, but to express a feeling, an emotion. Obviously, they turned to the most prestigious maker of incense in Japan, a small firm in Kyoto where production secrets have been handed down from generation to generation, and which has been supplying the imperial court for three centuries. Unfortunately, this company worked for the court exclusively, and had never made an incense based on someone else's idea. A meeting was finally accorded—after several months of waiting—only because the eminent incense maker was familiar with Mariage Frères, whose fame was already established in Japan and whose candles he had particularly appreciated. The rest was a question of mutual esteem and mutual instruction. A long dialogue ensued between the realm of Japanese incense and the world of French tea. During this period, Desains slowly came to understand exactly what it was he was seeking. And the emperor's incense manufacturer finally agreed, for the first time in the company's history, to make an incense whose scent was not of its own devising and which would not bear its name.

The development of the three fragrances required a great number of preliminary trials, which were the object of strictly codified "listening" sessions governed by the rules of *kodo,* "the way of incense." The participants, sitting in a circle in a room, each take in turn—in a particular way—a small pot where the incense is burning; they smell it by placing a hand in the smoke, at a given distance, and then pass it on to the next person in a precise gesture. Once the pot has gone around the entire circle, a conversation is held about what the incense "said."

It was during these many sessions, which allowed him to get ever closer to his original inspiration, that Desains was ultimately able to refine the final product. The three moments in the day of a tea garden could then be condensed into slim sticks, only to be liberated in the form of fragrant smoke.

Dawn-like sensations are embodied in the gray-colored stick, called Thé sous les Nuages (Tea and Clouds); the brick-red stick evokes the blaze of midday, called Bois de Thé (Tea and Wood); and night prowls forth in the form of the dark blue stick, Thé de Lune (Tea and Moonlight). Together, they virtually re-create an aromatic sojourn on a tea estate. Made by hand according to age-old methods, with highly rare plant resins but without the shaft of bamboo or wood found in ordinary incense (which alters the scent), they finally incarnate Desains and Sangmanee's old dream. Desains went on to design their packaging—a small, flat rectangular box in which the bundle of sticks is wrapped in black paper, accompanied by a silver-plated incense burner in the form of the old Mariage Frères shop sign. This pure, highly elegant case was not just a simple imitation of traditional Japanese boxes, much less a copy of Indian or Chinese packets, but a pure creation in the Mariage Frères spirit, which delighted the Kyoto manufacturer. The three fragrances first went on sale in 1999. And disappeared fast—they literally went up in smoke as soon as they hit the counters.

This instant popularity inspired Sangmanee and Desains to go further. When traveling in tea-growing regions, their minds and senses are always alert to new ideas for incense. And these ideas have become more and more abstract as they go further down the path of *kodo.* Whereas the first three scents re-created specific odors, subsequent ideas, although still linked to the world of tea, evoke—in the manner of Baudelairean correspondences—a series of sensations, settings, and images from the past. When visiting the Forbidden City in Beijing, seeing the eighteen monumental gilded bronze incense-holders standing on the terrace of the Palace of Supreme Harmony, they imagined the imperial residence in the days when it was wrapped, day and night, in a fragrant cloud created by thousands of sticks of incense, accompanied by the rustle and shimmer of silks worn by courtiers and mandarins. This image of a fragrance from a bygone era of extreme refinement ultimately gave birth to Thé Interdit (Forbidden Tea): musky, flowery, and silky like court gowns, grayish green like certain brocaded fabrics.

Thé au Tibet, meanwhile, re-created the impression of colors, smells, and smiles associated with the serenity of Buddhist temples in Tibet, especially at tea time. These sticks are saffron-colored, obviously, and give off a woody, honeyed, sweet fragrance conducive to meditation. And it was while working on the series of "tea calligraphy" canisters that Sangmanee and Desains had the idea for an Encre de Thé, or "Ink and Tea," incense. These black sticks give off a scent that evokes, on the one hand, the smells of a calligraphy workshop (the acidity of ink wed to the floral spiciness of black tea) and, on the other, the mental and aesthetic universe of artists of the brush.

This range of incense, first produced in 2001, also included two scents more directly related to tea: Terres de Thé evoked a tea estate in late summer, with its smell of damp earth and flowers, while Thé après l'Orage is a re-creation of a rain-drenched garden "after the storm," when all the vegetation has come alive and rejoices. The new incense sticks were of course produced by the same Japanese firm. And it is perhaps in Japan where Sangmanee and Desains were most thrilled by the international success of their incense. In a land where incense is increasingly associated with old-fashioned tradition and a bygone era, where a smoking stick is associated with old folks, young people began snapping up Thé Interdit and Bois de Thé! That is how the art of incense, rejuvenated and reconceived in the French manner by Mariage Frères, once again appealed to Japanese youth. Just one more proof, if proof were needed, of the universal appeal of the world's most inventive tea merchant.

7

TEA AND CUISINE

LEFT *Another Mariage Frères invention:*
Matcha salt, a blend of powdered Matcha tea and salt.
PRECEDING PAGES *Tea jelly—which now exists in nine*
flavors—was the first tea-based delicacy to be found
in Mariage Frères tearooms. The popularity of this jelly
and the pastries that followed encouraged the firm to invent
an entire tea-based cuisine, including savory dishes.

F rench cuisine associated tea with gastronomy at an early date. In the late eighteenth century, the great culinary expert Grimod de la Reynière already mentioned the gourmet possibilities of tea. "It is now received wisdom in Paris that teas cannot be offered without a dozen plates of light pastries. Ladies, young people, and children fall avidly upon them, for all ages enjoy these delicacies, which accord with all tastes and delight all stomachs." At that time, after more than a century of drinking green tea, Europe was discovering black tea, and it is a good bet that French gourmets were soon expert in matching the right pastries to the different varieties of tea. Strangely, only a few people thought of inventing gourmet delights made *with* tea, using it as an aromatic ingredient in a dish rather than just a beverage. Vincent La Chapelle was the only chef to suggest, in his *Cuisinier Moderne* of 1742, a recipe for tea-flavored cream. Two centuries later, the encyclopedic *Dictionnaire Larousse du XXᵉ Siècle* was still claiming that this cream was the only possible culinary composition based on tea.

The famous dictionary should nevertheless have mentioned the original invention of one Henri Mariage. In 1860, he flavored chocolate with tea and marketed it as Chocolat des Mandarins. The same Henri Mariage also devised a sweet tea jelly, but the Larousse was quite right to overlook this item because Mariage never put it on the market. Whatever the case, when Richard Bueno and Kitti Cha Sangmanee were inventing the French art of tea in the early 1980s, no French cook or pastry chef was using tea as an ingredient. The extremely subtle aromatic plant, with its magnificent palette of grassy, floral, fruity flavors, was strangely overlooked despite a long French tradition of blending tastes and ingredients. The anomaly struck the two men, who were seeking the most refined, gourmet way to teach the French to love tea. So when they opened their tearoom on Rue du Bourg-Tibourg in 1986, they were already thinking of turning it into a restaurant that featured tea-based cuisine. Obviously, it would have been simpler to remain content with a conventional tearoom that served a "five o'clock" tea accompanied by little cucumber sandwiches, scones, muffins, and marmalade. Also simpler, and probably more profitable in the short run, the lunch menu could have featured a few good Asian dishes, accompanied by a few cups of tea. But the pair of tea enthusiasts were not happy with these conventional ideas, which would contribute nothing to their concept of French tea connoisseurship.

At first, this new cuisine remained a dream. They were not chefs themselves, and their early contacts with professionals convinced them that the time was not yet ripe. French cooks, still unfamiliar with tea, were not ready to leap into the unknown. The Dutchman Bueno and the Thai Sangmanee often heard their queries answered by, "French cuisine with tea? What on earth is that?" So they decided to proceed in stages. The first step, when the tearoom-and-restaurant initially opened, was to elaborate a lunch menu comprised of light and inventive French dishes that would go well with tea; afternoon tea, meanwhile was accompanied by a list of sweet, tea-based treats. Thus right from 1986, luncheon customers were sampling some of the dishes that have become great Mariage Frères classics, still on the menu today although not employing tea as an ingredient—a "snob salad," for example, (which created a scandal at the time because it combined salmon with foie gras), or an open-faced smoked salmon sandwich, both of which can be marvelously accompanied by either a smoky tea or a green tea.

Afternoon tea, meanwhile, afforded Sangmanee and Bueno the opportunity, right from the first year, to present their first true tea-based condiment. It was a new version—slightly less sweet, and now flavored with rose—of Henri Mariage's tea jelly. The jelly was prepared fresh every morning in a large copper pot, and served in the restaurant that afternoon to accompany scones and muffins. The amazing popularity of this condiment, the first of its kind anywhere in the world, soon prompted Desains to bring out an entire range of nine jellies, sold in little glass jars in the retail outlet. Each was flavored with one of the firm's grand teas, such as Earl Grey Impérial, Marco Polo, and Eros. Encouraged by this success, the men finally decided to concoct tea-based pastries. Early inspirations were obviously indebted to Sangmanee's other explorations—an Earl Gray–flavored madeleine would never have seen the light of day if Mariage Frères hadn't been in the process of reinventing bergamot-scented teas, nor would the powdered Matcha tea cookie have occurred to them if the company hadn't been introducing the culture of green Japan tea into France. The cookie in particular, based on a traditional sweet called a *financier*, was especially bold: how would the French react to the bright green color and the unusual—for France—grassy taste? Sangmanee's passion for Matcha convinced him that he could introduce it as an ingredient in French cuisine, but the French themselves, who were only just discovering this exotic tea, had to be convinced. The green-tea *financier* turned out to be a hit, and encouraged Sangmanee to take the leap into savory dishes.

One of the first tea-based lunchtime dishes on the Mariage Frères menu was salmon with green Matcha tea, served with Siamese rice. It has now become one of the restaurant's old standbys. Guided by Sangmanee, the restaurant's chefs, Sébastien Delmas and Daniel Milliner, became increasingly accustomed to the idea of using tea in their dishes, and were soon extending the range of teas they were able to exploit, employing the whole gamut of harvests and blends. They learned to enliven a dish with a Chandernagor or Noël blend, to season white-fleshed fish with a scented green tea or an Earl Grey, to add

a dash of Darjeeling or a jasmine tea to fowl. Foie gras could even be accompanied by a tea jelly. All the fragrant nuances of the new spice were systematically mobilized. It first entered into the composition of sauces, creams, and salad dressings, then was added directly to fish dishes (in dry-leaf form) and salads (in infused-leaf form, notably a green China tea called Taiping Houkui). Then came the "tea mill," namely a pepper mill filled with tea leaves, to add a touch of flavor. Next came other green condiments that provided an original touch of color as well as flavor—Matcha Salt (a mixture of salt and green tea), Jade Powder (also made with Matcha tea, to accompany sweet dishes), and Green-tea Sesame to sprinkle over vegetables, pasta dishes, and sauces.

Nowadays, ninety-eight percent of the dishes on the menus of the four Mariage Frères restaurants contain tea. Because the chefs have six hundred teas at their disposal, they are constantly discovering new harmonies. In addition to the regular menu—which changes every season—at least one totally original dish is proposed to insatiably curious diners every week, becoming a key feature of the fixed-price "Lunch Tea" menu. Thus at least forty new tea-based dishes—and often many more—are created by Mariage Frères chefs every year. Since its launch in 1996, the "Lunch Tea" menu has spurred the creation of some eight hundred new recipes. The fixed-price deal includes a main course, a pot of tea, and a pastry dessert, and is inspired by the arrival of seasonal produce on the market. It also serves as the main testing ground for new taste combinations. As a rule, the main course will first be concocted by the chefs, then presented to Sangmanee, Desains, and Philippe Cohen-Tanugi. During the tasting session, each member of the jury is free to approve or to suggest slight changes—but the Mariage Frères chefs are now so experienced in handling the new ingredient that they usually receive the jury's wholehearted congratulations. To cite just a few recent examples, using only fresh, seasonal produce the chefs have audaciously roasted lamb with juice made from the Prince Igor blend (green and black teas flavored with citrus fruit), have presented "Egyptian-style" pigeon wrapped in a Pharaoh sauce (fruity green tea), and have flavored a crab and shrimp mousse with dressing that bears hints of the vanilla, spice, and mallow found in the Surabaya blend of red tea. The chefs' creativity and imagination is restrained by just one golden rule—the dish must be based on tea. The tea must never be swamped by the flavor of the main ingredient; on the contrary, the latter must enhance the former. The dish should allow the tea to express itself fully. That is exactly how,

in a gastronomic tradition stretching back to the Middle Ages, French cuisine has constantly reinvented itself with ingredients of exotic origin. Mariage Frères is indeed respecting French cuisine, with its sauces and creams, its hot and cold decoctions of herbs and seasonings, its careful presentation of portions on the plate. Yet the goal is not a stuffy "haute cuisine," but just a new and creative, light and colorful way to appreciate tea. Tea cuisine is also an innovative way to discover new flavors, new sensations, new horizons. Launched by Mariage Frères in the mid-1980s and subsequently adopted by tea lovers and food lovers alike, this cuisine has now received kudos from the press all over the world.

The same applies to Mariage Frères' cakes and pastries. Developed simultaneously with the main dishes, served as a dessert or as a tea-time snack, these inventive and delicious pastries have also become highly popular. Beginning with the Earl Grey madeleine and the Matcha *financier*, the list of tea-based pastries took on real scope with the arrival of pastry-chef Philippe Langlois, who worked closely with the Mariage Frères team to develop what has become the linchpin of all the tearooms today, namely the pastry cart. It is sometimes called the "Colonial Cart" because, in addition to scones, madeleines, and macaroons eaten with tea-flavored jellies, it features such treats as a "tarte coup de soleil" made with Bourbon-blend tea, tarts made with Matcha or Darjeeling tea, and pastry creams with exotic teas. But the firm's pastry range is not limited to these regular favorites. Just like the lunch menu, the dessert menu changes every season, with original treats proposed every three months. Although there is no question of removing classics like Splendeur du Tibet or Marco Polo Crème Brulée from the menu, summertime may bring additions such as fruit desserts brightened by a splash of Darjeeling (from the Mandakotee estate) and ice creams and sherbets flavored with famous blends of tea (Nil Rouge, Montagne d'Or, Métis).

Winter, meanwhile, will focus on appropriate fruit such as apples, pears, and oranges, bolstered by the warm and comforting flavor of teas such as a chocolaty Wedding Impérial, a stimulating Assam Sankar, or a velvety Earl Grey French Blue. Such creativity is now being exported to Japan, where Langlois regularly travels in order to train the pastry chef at the Mariage Frères restaurant in Ginza.

One new habit imported into France—what the French now call *le brunch*—greatly helped to familiarize people with tea-based cuisine. It was Mariage Frères who first introduced a brunch menu at its Bourg-Tibourg tearoom back in 1986. Having brunch at Mariage Frères on Saturday or Sunday morning swiftly became the height of Paris chic (and still is today). A relaxed weekend morning seemed conducive to the leisurely exploration of a new and unusual cuisine, and an increasing number of Parisians took the plunge. Not that they were forced to do so, for the savory dishes—fish, seafood, or fowl flavored with tea, or scrambled eggs with Matcha Salt—were simply offered alongside standard fare such as pastry, scones, muffins, and toast with tea jellies. Once on the menu, though, these subtle and charmingly colorful savory dishes wound up seducing even the most reticent of customers, who suddenly discovered a new range of delights.

Finally, it was inevitable that the victory of tea-based cuisine would be celebrated French-style, with a toast. And to drink to victory, Mariage Frères devised a range of six tea cocktails. These cold drinks, which can be sampled at all Mariage Frères establishments, reflect the same careful elaboration, high-quality ingredients, and imaginative blend of flavors found in the firm's teas and cuisine. Once again, it was not simply a question of adding another tea-based product to the list, but of seeking to bring out all the potential qualities of tea in a new and specifically French manner. To cite just three, whether the cocktail is called Mousse de Jade (cold liquid yogurt with Matcha tea), Luna Rossa (fresh grapefruit juice with "red moon" tea), or simply "Mariage's" (sparkling white wine with fruity Boléro tea—the only alcoholic version), each constitutes a perfect toast to Mariage Frères' successful worldwide mission: a lively, all-embracing love of tea.

ICED TEA
Ā LA MARIAGE FRÈRES

Mariage Frères recommends three methods for making a quart of iced tea:

- 1 -

To make strong iced tea, place 10 grams (four teaspoons) of tea in a teapot,
pour in half a quart of simmering water, and let steep for three
to five minutes, depending on the type of tea. Then remove the tea leaves
and pour the hot tea into glasses filled with ice cubes.

- 2 -

To make a lighter tea, almost like scented water, place 10 grams
(four teaspoons) of tea in a teapot or jug and add a quart of lukewarm water.
Then refrigerate for twelve hours. Strain the tea leaves before serving.

- 3 -

For Matcha—powdered green Japan tea—place 12 grams
(3 to 4 teaspoons) of tea in a wide bowl, add 10 cl. (half a cup) of simmering
water, beat with a whisk, then add more hot water, whipping constantly,
until a light mousse is obtained. Pour into a glass filled with ice cubes.

VINAIGRETTE
WITH SMOKY TARRY SOUCHONG TEA

(pictured opposite top right)

Serves 4

1/2 CUP SHERRY VINEGAR

1/4 OZ. TARRY SOUCHONG TEA (2 LEVEL TABLESPOONS)

3/4 CUP SUNFLOWER OIL

1 TEASPOON MUSTARD

SALT, PEPPER

In a bowl, mix together the vinegar and the tea. Season with salt and pepper,
add the mustard, and gradually whip in the oil. Strain.
This recipe can be made with teas other than Tarry Souchong
(pictured opposite, top right)—such as green Matcha tea (bottom left).
However, it is important to use ingredients that complement each other.
For example, when making the vinaigrette with Lune Rouge tea (top left),
use distilled vinegar and omit the mustard.
When making the vinaigrette with red Métis tea (bottom right),
use raspberry vinegar.
For best results, the tea should be steeped in the vinegar
for 12 hours before final preparation.

STEAMED COD
WITH GREEN-TEA SESAME, MATCHSTICK LEEKS,
SUN-DRIED TOMATOES, AND CHIVE OIL

Serves 4

4 COD FILLETS ABOUT 1/4 LB. EACH

6 LEEKS

DASH OF SESAME-SEED OIL

GREEN-TEA SESAME

16 SLICES SUN-DRIED TOMATOES

2/3 CUP SUNFLOWER OIL

1 BUNCH CHIVES, CHOPPED

SALT, PEPPER

Mix the sunflower oil with the chopped chives in a blender. Season with salt
and pepper, strain. Wash and trim the leeks, cut in half crosswise and then slice each section
lengthwise into quarters. Steam the cod fillets. Meanwhile, poach the leeks in boiling salted
water, drain, transfer to a bowl, and moisten with a dash of sesame-seed oil. Arrange the leeks
on serving plates and top with the slices of sun-dried tomato.
Add the cod fillets, sprinkle with the Green-tea Sesame, and moisten with the chive oil.

Recommended tea
A flowery, fresh, slightly fruity first-flush Darjeeling tea
(Ambootia, Namring Upper, or Jungpana).

FILLETS OF RED MULLET
IN BOUDDHA BLEU TEA INK
WITH BEET CHIPS

Serves 4

4 RED MULLET	**FOR THE SAUCE**
ABOUT 1 LB. EACH,	**1 TABLESPOON BOUDDHA BLEU**
SCALED AND FILLETED	**TEA LEAVES**
2 BEETS, PRE-COOKED	**1/4 CUP SUGAR SYRUP**
2 TABLESPOONS FLOUR	**1/4 CUP LEMON JUICE**
1 QUART PEANUT OIL FOR DEEP-FAT FRYING	**1/4 CUP ORANGE JUICE**
CHERVIL LEAVES	**1/4 CUP SOY SAUCE**
OLIVE OIL	**2 TEASPOONS CUTTLEFISH INK**
SALT, PEPPER	**SALT, PEPPER**

Preparation of the deep-fried beet chips: Place the peanut oil in a deep-fat fryer and heat to 285°F (140°C). Peel the pre-cooked beets and cut into thin slices. Dredge in flour and deep fry one-by-one in the hot peanut oil. Remove the slices before they have time to color, drain on absorbent paper, season with salt. Preparation of the sauce: Heat the sugar syrup, add the Bouddha Bleu tea, lemon and orange juice, soy sauce, and cuttlefish ink. Season to taste and strain. Season the red mullet fillets with salt and pepper. Heat the olive oil and sauté the fillets for 3 minutes on each side. Pour a base of sauce into the serving plates and top with a fan of red mullet fillets. Garnish with the deep-fried beet chips, sprinkle with the chervil leaves.

Recommended teas
A green Japan tea, either brisk and somewhat grassy (such as Sencha Yame or Kawanecha) or lightly toasted (such as Hojicha).

SCALLOPS WITH LUNE ROUGE TEA

Serves 4

20 SCALLOPS

24 BABY FENNEL BULBS

1 AND 1/2 TABLESPOONS FRESH GINGER, GRATED

3/4 CUP DISTILLED VINEGAR

1 AND 1/2 CUPS OLIVE OIL

1/3 OZ. LUNE ROUGE TEA (2 TABLESPOONS)

2 TABLESPOONS BUTTER

2 TABLESPOONS GRANULATED (CASTOR) SUGAR

SALT, PEPPER

The day before: combine the vinegar and tea in a blender and mix briefly.
Chill for at least 12 hours. After the vinegar-and-tea mixture has chilled for 12 hours or more,
blend again for 2 minutes while gradually adding the olive oil. Season the vinaigrette with salt
and pepper, set aside. Poach the fennel bulbs in boiling salted water. Beat the vinaigrette
with a wire whip. Strain, pressing well, and add the ginger. Sauté the scallops in the butter.
Remove the scallops from the pan and sauté the poached fennel in the remaining butter.
Arrange the scallops and fennel on serving plates, moisten with the vinaigrette.

Recommended tea
A brisk, slightly woody blue tea (Ti Kwan Yin Supreme from China with its hint of white flowers,
or Thai Beauty with its scent of magnolia and note of peach).

SAUTEED FILLETS OF PIKE PERCH
GLAZED WITH ORIENTAL TEA,
ON A BED OF GREEN ASPARAGUS
AND SNOW PEAS

Serves 4

4 FILLETS OF PIKE PERCH

ABOUT 1/4 LB. EACH

OLIVE OIL

20 GREEN ASPARAGUS SPEARS

1/4 LB. SNOW PEAS

2 OZ. GREEN PEAS

SALT, PEPPER

FOR THE SAUCE

1 TABLESPOON ORIENTAL FLAVORED TEA LEAVES

4 TABLESPOONS SUGAR

4 TABLESPOONS WATER

DASH BALSAMIC VINEGAR

3/4 CUP TOMATO PURÉE

1 TABLESPOON GARLIC, CHOPPED

1 TABLESPOON FRESH GINGER, CHOPPED

DASH OF OLIVE OIL

SALT, PEPPER

Poach the vegetables in boiling salted water until done but still crunchy. Refresh in iced water and drain. Preparation of the sauce: Caramelize the water and sugar, deglaze with balsamic vinegar and reduce by one-half. Add the tomato purée, chopped garlic, ginger, and olive oil. Simmer this mixture over low heat until it forms a glaze. Add the Oriental tea and steep for 2 minutes. Strain. Season the fillets of pike perch with salt and pepper, sauté in hot olive oil for 6 minutes on each side. Pour a base of sauce into the serving plates, top with the fillets of pike perch and garnish with the asparagus spears and green peas. Finish with a fan of snow peas.

Recommended tea
A green, wok-made Burma tea (Ko Kant, with its sweet, grassy bouquet and hint of flowers).

SALMON WITH GREEN MATCHA TEA

Serves 4

2 SALMON FILLETS, BONED AND SKINNED	4 GREEN ASPARAGUS SPEARS
4 BABY TURNIPS	1 SHALLOT, CHOPPED
8 BABY CARROTS	3/4 CUP FISH STOCK
8 SPRING ONIONS	2/3 CUP LIGHT CREAM
8 BABY YELLOW SQUASH	1 KNOB BUTTER
1/4 LB. SNOW PEAS, TRIMMED	1 TEASPOON GREEN MATCHA TEA

Poach all the vegetables in boiling salted water. When done but still crunchy, refresh in ice water.
Butterfly-cut the salmon fillets by inserting a knife and gently slicing crosswise,
leaving the two slices attached on one side. Place the salmon fillets on a flat surface, open,
and press flat. Season with salt and pepper, sprinkle with the Matcha tea. Roll the fillets
into cylinders and wrap tightly in plastic film. Sauté the shallot in butter until soft but not colored,
add the fish stock, and boil until reduced to a few tablespoons. Add the cream and reduce again
until the sauce is thick enough to coat a spoon. Whip in the Matcha tea. Strain the sauce
and keep warm. Unwrap the salmon cylinders and steam until done. Reheat the poached
vegetables over boiling water or stir-fry in a sauté pan or wok with a little water, butter, and salt.
Stir constantly until all the vegetables are shiny and golden. Place the steamed salmon fillets
on serving plates, surround with the vegetables, and garnish with a ribbon of the Matcha sauce.

Recommended teas
A white tea from China (the smooth yet brisk Pai Mu Tan Impérial) or Darjeeling
(Ambootia's Pivoine d'Himalaya with its hint of green almond and wildflowers).

OPIUM HILL LANGOUSTINES

Serves 4

20 LANGOUSTINES, SHELLED

1/4 LB. YOUNG LEAFY SPINACH

1 MANGO

1/2 BUNCH FLAT PARSLEY

1/2 BUNCH CHERVIL

1/2 BUNCH DILL

1/2 HEAD CURLY LETTUCE

1 CUP SOY SAUCE

3/4 CUP SESAME-SEED OIL

1 TEASPOON OLIVE OIL

1/3 OZ. OPIUM HILL TEA LEAVES (2 TABLESPOONS)

SALT, PEPPER

The day before: place the tea leaves in a small bowl, cover with cold water, refrigerate, and allow to steep for at least 12 hours. Three or four hours before final preparation, reduce the soy sauce by boiling until it forms a caramel-like syrup. Chill. Peel the mango and cut into even crescent-shaped slices. Wash the spinach, set aside. Wash and drain the herbs, remove the leaves from the stems and mix together. Drain the tea leaves without squeezing, add to the herb mixture, and blend with the sesame-seed oil and a little salt. Set aside. Arrange a fan of mango slices and spinach leaves on one side of the serving plates. Decorate with a zigzag of the caramelized soy sauce. Sauté the langoustines in the olive oil until thoroughly cooked. Place a mound of the herb mixture on the other side of the serving plates, garnish with the langoustines.

Recommended teas

A green tea made in the Chinese fashion (the mild yet flowery Huan Shan Mao Feng, or Taiping Houkui with its fragrance of orchids, or Champasak from Laos with its intense aroma and slightly smoky taste).

FILLET OF DUCK WITH TEA JELLY
AND MARCO POLO TEA

Serves 4

2 DUCK FILLETS

1 CUP VEAL STOCK

3/4 CUP RASPBERRY VINEGAR

1/3 CUP MARCO POLO TEA JELLY

3 LARGE GRANNY SMITH APPLES

2 TABLESPOONS MARCO POLO TEA

1 TABLESPOON GRANULATED (CASTOR) SUGAR

1 KNOB BUTTER

SALT, PEPPER

Preheat oven to 400°F (200°C). Remove excess fat from the duck fillets and cut a cross-hatch
pattern on the surface of the skin without cutting through to the flesh. Place the vinegar
and tea jelly in a small pan over medium heat and reduce, stirring, until thickened.
Deglaze with the veal stock and reduce again until the sauce is dark and lustrous.
Add the Marco Polo tea, remove from heat, and allow to steep covered for at least 4 minutes.
Strain the sauce and keep warm. Sauté the duck fillets over high heat for about 2 minutes
on each side, transfer to an ovenproof pan and bake for 6-8 minutes. Meanwhile, peel the apples,
cut into quarters, and sauté in the butter over high heat. Turn after 30 seconds,
season with the salt, pepper, and sugar. Turn again. Place a mound of apples
on the serving plates. Slice the duck fillets and arrange in a fan shape next to the apples.
Garnish with a ribbon of the tea sauce.

Recommended teas
A whole-leaf, non-smoky China tea (the sweet, mild Roi du Keemun, or the fine
and flowery Yunnan Impérial), an Assam tea (the malty, spicy Numalighur),
or even a Darjeeling (a round, full-bodied second flush from Margaret's Hope).

MATCHA TEA POUND CAKE

8 OZ. BUTTER

8 OZ. CONFECTIONERS' (ICING) SUGAR

5 EGGS

8 OZ. (PLAIN) FLOUR

2 TEASPOONS BAKING POWDER

1/2 OZ. GREEN MATCHA UJI TEA (4 TEASPOONS)

Preheat oven to 300°F (150°C). Allow the butter to soften at room temperature.
Cream the softened butter with the sugar until smooth and light-colored. Separate the eggs,
add the yolks to the butter mixture and beat until thoroughly blended. Add the flour,
baking powder, and green Matcha Uji tea. Beat until blended. Whip the five egg whites until firm.
Stir a little of the beaten egg whites into the cake batter and then gently fold in the rest.
Butter two small bread tins and line with ovenproof paper. Fill three-quarters full with the cake batter
and bake for about 40 minutes, or until the point of a sharp knife inserted into the middle of
the cakes comes out clean. Allow the cakes to rest for a few minutes before removing from the pans.

Recommended teas
Any tea from the range of flavored blends: fruity, flowery,
malty or flavored with vanilla and spices.

ACKNOWLEDGEMENTS

The author warmly thanks Kitti Cha Sangmanee, Franck Desains,
and Philippe Cohen-Tanugi who, with an extraordinary generosity,
opened the doors of Mariage Frères, offering a precious
amount of their time as well as the tasting of sublime teas.
He also thanks all of those who welcomed and informed him
in the firm's various establishments, in particular Laurent Sonnino,
Bruno Combes, Mikitake Ushida, Brahim Kebir, Miguel Chevalier,
David Chavanne, Sébastien Delmas, Daniel Milliner,
Xavier Travers and Claudia Mingori. Together they make Mariage Frères
a firm of an exceptional human wealth.

LEFT *19th century painted wood tea container used by Mariage Frères to import Lapsong Souchong.*
Tea Museum, Mariage Frères, Paris.

PHOTOGRAPHIC SOURCES

All the photography in this volume is by Francis Hammond, except the following:

p. 14: Jean-Pierre Dieterlen/Mariage Frères; p. 17: Mariage Frères Tea Museum; p. 21: Mariage Frères Tea Museum; p. 24: Mariage Frères Tea Museum; p. 25; Mariage Frères Tea Museum; pp. 28-29: Mariage Frères Tea Museum; p. 32: Mariage Frères Tea Museum; p. 47: Jean-Pierre Dieterlen/Mariage Frères; pp. 52, 53, 54: Mariage Frères; p. 58: Franck Desains/Mariage Frères; pp. 60, 61, 62, 63: Mariage Frères Tea Museum; p. 64: Franck Desains/Mariage Frères; p. 65: Mariage Frères Tea Museum; p. 67: Jean-Pierre Dieterlen/Mariage Frères; p. 69: Franck Desains/Mariage Frères; pp. 70-75 (the photographs reproduced in the albums): Franck Desains/Mariage Frères; p. 77 (left): Franck Desains/Mariage Frères; (right): Kitti Cha Sangmanee; p. 78: Franck Desains/Mariage Frères; p. 81: Franck Desains/Mariage Frères; pp. 82-85 (the photographs reproduced in the albums): Franck Desains/Mariage Frères; p. 87: Franck Desains/Mariage Frères; p. 88: Franck Desains/Mariage Frères; p. 89: Franck Desains/Mariage Frères; p. 91: Franck Desains/Mariage Frères; p. 92: Franck Desains/Mariage Frères; p. 95: Franck Desains/Mariage Frères; pp. 96-97 (the photographs reproduced in the albums): Richard Bueno/Mariage Frères; pp. 98-101 (the photographs reproduced in the albums): Franck Desains/Mariage Frères; p. 148: Jean-Pierre Dieterlen/Mariage Frères; pp. 150-151: Bénédicte Petit/Mariage Frères; p. 153: Art2Link; pp. 160-161: Jean-Pierre Dieterlen/Mariage Frères; pp. 166-167: Jean-Pierre Dieterlen/Mariage Frères; p. 174: Jean-Pierre Dieterlen/Mariage Frères; p. 175: Philippe Chancel; p. 178: Jean-Pierre Dieterlen/Mariage Frères; p. 186: Mariage Frères Tea Museum; p. 193: Jean-Pierre Dieterlen/Mariage Frères; p. 207: Mariage Frères Tea Museum; p. 238: Mariage Frères Tea Museum; p. 239: Mariage Frères Tea Museum; p. 240: Mariage Frères Tea Museum.

pp. 34, 42, 44, 66, 76, 79, 90, 107, 114, 120, 125, 133, 161, 173, 177, 192, 196, 201, 210 (engravings): Mariage Frères archives.